Diet Recipes and Tips
Volume 2

To read more on the entire HCG diet, please visit
www.YourHCG.com.

About Your HCG

YourHCG.com utilizes the highest standards to compliance protocols as well as manufacturing Kosher and Organic products. In addition, we provide homeopathic remedies that are made with individual care using traditional methods complying with current Good Manufacturing Practices (GMP). We implement high quality standards for the manufacturing of the remedies. Optimal reliability and reproducibility of the dilutions is guaranteed by the standardization of the manufacturing processes. Utilizing a time tested process, we rely on over 20 years of experience in the nutritional supplements field to produce top quality products.

Table of Contents

Dedication

Being overweight hurts more than just your physical appearance. It is linked to emotional issues, health issues, and much more. This book is dedicated to anyone on the HCG diet who needs a little more variety in his or her food choices.

Oftentimes, HCG dieters can find themselves being bored with the food they can have. In this book, you will find over 200 recipes and tips to help you. You will love the delicious recipes. Here's to a healthy life and a healthier you!

–Your HCG

The Diet Overview

Here are the program steps you will follow when using the Your HCG Diet Program:

1. *Read Dr. Simeons Pounds and Inches.* It can be found at www.yourhcg.com/poundsandinches.pdf.
2. Studies have shown that 6 INDIVIDUAL drops, 6 times per day is the most effective way to use the Your HCG product. This allows the HCG to be more constant in your system. It's best to start the drops when you wake up, and then spread them out every 2-3 hours.
3. Here is how to administer the drops for best absorption: While looking in the mirror, hold the dropper straight up and down. This is important to ensure the drops are the correct size. Holding the dropper at an angle can cause you to take bigger drops, allowing your bottle to run out faster than the listed time. Place 6 HCG drops under your tongue and let them sit for 15 seconds before swallowing. Then do not eat or drink anything for at least 30 minutes. You do not need to take your drops with food, and it is okay to eat immediately before taking your drops. The most important thing to remember is not to eat or drink anything for a minimum of 30 minutes AFTER taking your drops. If you have a dropper with the .5mL and 1mL marking, please disregard the markings. Continue to take 6 drops, 6 times per day.
4. Follow Dr. Simeons original diet protocol, which is also listed in this book.

5. Days 1 and 2 – Start taking your HCG drops and eat everything and anything! The more fat, the better. We know, it sounds crazy, but the drops take 48 hours to fully enter your system, and this will help significantly with hunger and energy during the next week. Eat foods that are saturated in fat i.e. whipping cream, butter soaked eggs, bacon, sausage, pizza, etc.

6. Day 3 – Start the low calorie diet protocol (also known as VLCD or phase 2). Continue the HCG drops for a minimum of 21 days and a maximum of 45 days. If you reach your goal weight before 23 days, please contact us for further instructions. Do NOT take the drops for more than 45 days. If you have additional weight to lose after the 45 days, please contact us for further instructions.

7. Continue the 500–calorie diet for 72 hours after your last dose of HCG. This is how long it will take for the HCG to be eliminated from your system. Use the weight the morning of your last dose for your weight to maintain during maintenance. For short, this is called your Last Dose Weight (LDW).

8. For at least 6 weeks after your last dose of HCG, follow the maintenance protocol (phase 3). Please see the maintenance guidelines below. You will increase your calorie intake but still avoid sugars and starches of any kind. For sugars, this means pure cane sugar and anything ending in –ose, maltodextrin, aspartame, etc. For starches, you will discontinue the Grissini breadstick and Melba toast. You'll also want to avoid rice, pasta, bread, wheat, potatoes, etc.

9. During maintenance if your weight goes over 2.0lbs from your LDW, you will need to do a steak day. If your weight goes under 2.0lbs from your LDW, you will need to increase your calorie intake.
10. Once you complete the first half of maintenance, very gradually add starches and sugars in small quantities, always controlled by morning weight. You'll continue adding in new sugars and starches until your weight stabilizes.
11. Maintenance will increase after each round of the HCG diet. Here is a guideline for maintenance:
    a) After round 1, you'll do a total of 6 weeks of maintenance – 3 weeks of no sugars/starches followed by 3 weeks of SLOWLY reintroducing sugars/starches.
    b) After round 2, you'll do a total of 8 weeks of maintenance – 4 weeks of no sugars/starches followed by 4 weeks of SLOWLY reintroducing sugars/starches.
    c) After round 3, you'll do a total of 12 weeks of maintenance – 6 weeks of no sugars/starches followed by 6 weeks of SLOWLY reintroducing sugars/starches.
    d) After round 4, you'll do a total of 20 weeks of maintenance – 10 weeks of no sugars/starches followed by 10 weeks of SLOWLY reintroducing sugars/starches.
    e) After round 5, you'll do a total of 6 months of maintenance – 3 months of no sugars/starches followed by 3 months of SLOWLY reintroducing sugars/starches.

The Diet Protocol

Breakfast:
- Black Coffee or
- Green Tea or
- Yerba Mate Tea or
- Wu Long Tea or
- Chamomile Tea

You may have as much as you desire. You may sweeten the tea and coffee with stevia, but no other sweeteners should be used. Make sure that the stevia doesn't contain any additional ingredients like erythritol, dextrose, maltodextrin, etc.

Lunch:
1. 100 grams (weighed raw) of one of the meat choices below. These choices should be grilled, baked or cooked without the use of oils or butter:
- Beef – This is not an ideal choice of protein. If you do have beef, limit it to a lean cut like Round Roast or London broil and only have beef 1–2 times per week.
- Veal
- Fresh white fish (should not be frozen) – Ayr, Cat Fish, Cod, Coley, Dover Sole, Flounder, Flying Fish, Haddock, Hake, Halibut, Hoki, John Dory, Kalabasu, Lemon Sole, Ling, Monk Fish, Parrot Fish, Plaice, Pollack, Pomfret, Red & Grey Mullet, Red Fish, Red Snapper, Rohu, Sea Bass, Sea Bream, Shark, Skate, Tilapia, Turbot, and Whiting. ** The best place to buy fresh fish would be a local health food store if you live in a land-locked state.

- Shellfish (shrimp, crab, prawn, lobster, etc.)
- Boneless, skinless chicken breast
- Very occasionally we allow eggs – boiled, poached or raw – to people who develop an aversion to meat. The serving size should be 1 whole egg and 3 egg whites. This option is best if only used 1–2 times per week.
- Your HCG Whey Protein Shake in Vanilla, Strawberry or Chocolate. This can be used 3–4 times per week as a protein replacement.

**(Per Pounds and Inches, American beef has almost double the caloric value of South Italian beef, which is not marbled with fat. The marbling is impossible to remove. In America, therefore, low-grade veal should be used for one meal and fish (excluding all those species such as herring, mackerel, tuna, salmon, eel, etc., which have a high fat content, and all dried smoked or pickled fish), chicken breast, lobster, crawfish, prawns, shrimps, crabmeat or kidneys for the other meal.

2. One large handful of one of the following vegetables:
- Spinach
- Chard
- Chicory
- Beet greens
- Lettuce of any kind
- Tomatoes
- Celery
- Fennel
- White, yellow or red onions
- Red radishes

- Cucumbers
- Asparagus
- Cabbage

These can be eaten raw, steamed, grilled, or boiled. You are allowed only one vegetable per meal. Do not mix vegetables.

3. One of the following fruits:
- 1 apple
- 1 orange
- 1/2 grapefruit
- 1 handful of strawberries
- Juice of 1 lemon in addition to the 2 fruit servings per day

4. One Grissini breadstick or one Melba toast.

Dinner:
You will pick 4 items from the items listed above. You can have one lean protein, one vegetable, one fruit, and one breadstick or Melba toast for both lunch and dinner.

Drinks Allowed:
Plain spring water, still mineral water, tea, coffee, Zevia. You should drink at least 2 liters of water per day. We actually recommend drinking 1/2 of your weight in ounces per day. For example, if you weigh 200lbs you'll want to drink a minimum of 100oz of water daily. Also you are allowed 1 TBSP of whole milk per 24-hour period.
** Zevia is not on the original protocol. Use at your own risk.

Seasonings Allowed:

Salt, pepper, white vinegar, apple cider vinegar, mustard powder, garlic powder, basil, parsley, thyme, marjoram, etc. Spices and herbs should be in their natural form for best results. Watch out for added sugar, artificial sweeteners, mixed veggies, or foods not allowed on the diet (i.e. carrots) in your spices!

Miscellaneous Tips for the HCG Diet

- You may eat the breadstick and fruit as a snack in between meals instead of with your meals if you choose.
- No over the counter non-prescription drugs should be taken (with the exception of Aspirin). ** Consult your physician before discontinuing any medications, prescription or non-prescription.
- No cosmetics other than lipstick, eyebrow pencil, and facial powder should be used. If you must use cosmetics, mineral makeup will not stall your loss.
- No creams, lotions, or moisturizers that contain fat should be used. (Check the ingredient list. You can stall your weight loss if the product contains oil (other than mineral oil) or has anything ending in -ose).
- Those not uncommon patients who feel that even so little food is too much for them, can omit anything they wish (page 31 in Pounds and Inches).
- Massages are not recommended while on the HCG diet (page 42 in Pounds and Inches).

It is encouraged, but not required to do the following:

- Go walking, do yoga, or swim for up to one hour per day, 3-5 times per week.
- Listen to stress reducing CDs.
- Sweat for 20 minutes in a sauna as often as possible.
- Get twenty minutes of sun daily.
- Do not drink very cold beverages.

The Vegetarian Diet Protocol

Breakfast:
- Black Coffee or
- Green Tea or
- Yerba Mate Tea or
- Wu Long Tea or
- Chamomile Tea

You may have as much as you desire. You may sweeten the tea and coffee with stevia, but no other sweeteners should be used. Make sure that the stevia doesn't contain any additional ingredients like erythritol, dextrose, maltodextrin, etc.

Lunch:
1. 100 grams (weighed raw) of one of the protein choices below. These choices should be grilled, baked or cooked without the use of oils or butter:
- 1 soy patty (not to exceed 110 calories)*
- ½ c. cooked quinoa*
- 8 oz. of unsweetened soy milk*
- 8 oz. of unsweetened hemp milk*
- 3.5 oz. of fat free cottage cheese* (this choice will slow your loss)
- YourHCG.com Whey Protein Shake (available in vanilla, chocolate or strawberry)

There have been many advancements since the original protocol was introduced. The shakes do include the following ingredients: Whey protein, natural and artificial flavors, xanthan gum**, stevia**, and soy lecithin**.

*Not on the original protocol, may slow or stall loss.

**Not on the original protocol, but are HCG friendly.

2. One large handful of one of the following vegetables:
- Spinach
- Chard
- Chicory
- Beet greens
- Lettuce of any kind
- Tomatoes
- Celery
- Fennel
- White, yellow or red onions
- Red radishes
- Cucumbers
- Asparagus
- Cabbage

These can be eaten raw, steamed, grilled or boiled. You are allowed only one vegetable per meal. Do not mix vegetables.

3. One of the following fruits:
- 1 apple
- 1 orange
- 1/2 grapefruit
- 1 handful of strawberries
- Juice of 1 lemon in addition to the 2 fruit servings per day

4. One Grissini breadstick or one Melba toast.

Dinner:
You will pick 4 items from the items listed above. You can have one lean protein, one vegetable, one fruit, and one breadstick or Melba toast for both lunch and dinner.

The Vegan Diet Protocol

Breakfast:
- Black Coffee or
- Green Tea or
- Yerba Mate Tea or
- Wu Long Tea or
- Chamomile Tea

You may have as much as you desire. You may sweeten the tea and coffee with stevia, but no other sweeteners should be used. Make sure that the stevia doesn't contain any additional ingredients like erythritol, dextrose, maltodextrin, etc.

Lunch:
1. 100 grams (weighed raw) of one of the protein choices below. These choices should be grilled, baked or cooked without the use of oils or butter:
- 1 soy patty (not to exceed 110 calories)*
- ½ c. cooked quinoa*
- 8 oz. of unsweetened soy milk*
- 8 oz. of unsweetened hemp milk*

*Not on the original protocol, may slow or stall loss.

2. One large handful of one of the following vegetables:
- Spinach
- Chard
- Chicory
- Beet greens
- Lettuce of any kind
- Tomatoes

- Celery
- Fennel
- White, yellow or red onions
- Red radishes
- Cucumbers
- Asparagus
- Cabbage

These can be eaten raw, steamed, grilled or boiled. You are allowed only one vegetable per meal. Do not mix vegetables.

3. One of the following fruits:
- 1 apple
- 1 orange
- 1/2 grapefruit
- 1 handful of strawberries
- Juice of 1 lemon in addition to the 2 fruit servings per day

4. One Grissini breadstick or one Melba toast.

Dinner:
You will pick 4 items from the items listed above. You can have one lean protein, one vegetable, one fruit, and one breadstick or Melba toast for both lunch and dinner.

Plateau Breakers and Weight Loss Maximizers

If you hit a plateau, which is considered no weight loss OR inches lost in at least 4 days, here are some suggestions to help you get over it. (These tips can also help maximize your weight loss!)

- Increase water intake to 2-3 quarts per day. You want to drink 1/2 your weight in water per day. So if you weigh 200lbs, you'll drink 100oz of water per day.
- Try adding a glass or 2 of home-brewed green tea to your day.
- Don't eat 2 apples for the two fruits or cut down on the size of the apples. Adding variety to your diet will help maximize your weight loss.
- American beef is fatty. Cut it down or out completely. Seafood and chicken are much better choices.
- Check all condiments for any form of sugar.
- If mixing vegetables, stop.
- Try adding up to 4 TBSP of apple cider vinegar to your daily routine. Make an Apple Cider Vinegar Cocktail - In a glass mix 8oz of water, 1 dropper of stevia, juice of ½ lemon, and 2 TBSP of vinegar. Drink twice per day.
- Grapefruit is a known fat burner; choose this as one of your fruits for the day.

- Taking potassium supplements can help you lose weight. Potassium helps release fluid from the cells. Always consult your physician before adding in any new supplements.
- Try leaving out one or both bread sticks or Melba toast.
- Make sure you are not drinking any "diet" drinks. Any form of sugar or "non-sugar" besides stevia will slow your weight loss.
- Try not to eat anything from suppertime until lunch the next day. Studies have shown that people on the diet lose more by skipping breakfast. (Still drink fluids!)
- Try cutting down the amount of coffee and mint you are consuming. They can decrease your body's response to homeopathic products.

Apple Day

This is a method used on the low calorie diet to help break a plateau. It is very important to be aware that it is common to experience a stall in weight loss lasting a few days on the HCG diet. Don't worry; your weight loss will continue again. Do NOT do an apple day if you are near or on your menstrual cycle. Sticking to the diet, drinking plenty of water, and being patient are the best remedies for a stall. IF your stall has lasted 4 or more days, try the following apple day:

For one day, abstain from all foods with the exception of the following:

- 6 large apples of any variety
- Water to maintain hydration

You can find Dr. Simeons explanation of the apple day on Page 35 of Pounds and Inches under Plateaus.

Tips to Combat Hunger

If you are experiencing hunger, here is a chart to help you overcome your hunger or cravings:

1. How long have you been on the diet protocol?
Less than 8 days: It is very common to experience mild hunger the first few days. Make sure you are drinking plenty of water and following the diet exactly. The hunger will subside by about the 8th day.
More than 8 days: Go to question #2.

2. How much water are you drinking?
Less than half my weight in ounces of water per day: You need to be consuming at least half your weight in ounces per water every day. Example, if you weigh 200 pounds, you need to drink 100 ounces of water every day.
At least half my weight in ounces of water per day: Go to question #3.

3. Are you truly hungry? Is your tummy is growling? Or does that donut just look really good? :
I think I am just having cravings: Part of the diet is learning how to make better eating choices. Learning how to distinguish between cravings and hunger is a big part of the diet. You will soon learn that a strawberry can be just as rewarding as a donut. Please also see "additional tips below.
I really am hungry!: Go to question #4

4. You may need to increase your drops.
Try starting with 7 drops 6 times per day and see if this helps. Another way to help mild hunger cravings is by spreading your food throughout the day. For example, eat your "lunch fruit" at 10 A.M. and your "dinner fruit" at 3 P.M. You can also eat your melba toast as a snack throughout the day.

Here are some additional tips to help you overcome hunger, frustration, and even cravings:

1. *GUM* – Chew a piece of HCG approved gum. SteviaDent is a great choice and can be purchased at www.yourhcgshop.com.
2. *SPICES* – Spice up your diet! Instead of eating that tomato plain, try adding some Italian spices, vinegar, or salt and pepper. Spices are a great addition to almost any meal and will leave you feeling more satisfied, so your diet is not so bland. Use the recipes in this book to 'spice' up your diet.
3. *EGGS* – Dr. Simeons allows for the occasional use of eggs on the diet. You can have one whole egg and 3 egg whites to equal one serving of protein. So if you are bored of chicken, fish and red meat, make some eggs! You can even make an omelet containing your favorite vegetable (remember, this takes care of your vegetable and protein serving for one meal).
4. *BRUSH YOUR TEETH* – If all else fails, brush your teeth! We know it sounds crazy, but how often do you feel like eating after you've brushed your teeth?

5. *FACEBOOK* – If you are feeling frustrated, overwhelmed, or hungry, visit our Facebook page, www.facebook.com/yourhcg. We also have our Your HCG Community available at http://community.yourhcg.com/. There are thousands of fans on our Facebook page and on our community who are always there to give you support, encouragement, and tips.

6. **IMAGINATION** – Before you cheat and/or give up, picture yourself skinny! This can keep you motivated most of the time, and can prevent you from cheating. A lot of customers will hang up a picture of themselves before they started the diet to use as motivation. Post a picture in your bedroom or bathroom to give you the motivation to become a healthier person.

7. *WATER* – Drinking water, especially with lemon, is a great way to fight hunger. You will be surprised how full you feel after drinking a glass or 2 of water. Adding lemon helps with weight loss, decreases cravings, and provides you with some extra flavor. You are allowed the juice of 1 lemon per day in addition to your two fruit servings.

8. *GREEN TEA* – Green tea is proven to aid in weight loss efforts. It is also an appetite suppressant. Try it hot or cold, and add some stevia if you wish. Lemon flavored stevia is wonderful in green tea. Don't like tea? Get some green tea capsules at your local health food store; just make sure they are sugar free.

9. *SNACK!* – Most people love to snack! If you feel like you must snack while on the diet, here is a schedule to help you get through your day: 10 AM – Fruit, 12 PM – Veggie and Protein, 2 PM – Melba Toast, 5 PM – Veggie and Protein, 6 PM – Melba Toast, 8 PM– Fruit.

HCG Friendly Shopping List

Here is a list of items that will help you get prepared for the HCG diet and make your shopping trip a little easier!

- Boneless, skinless chicken breast
- Fish (crab, shrimp, tilapia, cod, etc.)
- London Broil, Round Roast and Veal
- Lemons
- Apples
- Oranges
- Strawberries
- Grapefruit
- Cabbage
- Asparagus
- Cucumbers
- Radishes
- Onions
- Celery
- Tomatoes
- Lettuce
- Spinach
- Melba Toast and/or Grissini Breadsticks
- Stevia (check ingredients for anything ending in –ose, maltodextrin, etc.)
- Apple Cider Vinegar
- Green Tea
- Letter Scale for weighing food
- Digital Scale for weighing yourself
- Water bottle (so you know how much water you drink daily)

Low Calorie Diet Recipes

Beverages (11)

STRAWBERRY MARGARITA (minus tequila)
1 c. of strawberries
Juice of ½ lemon
1 ½ packets of stevia
4-5 ice cubes

Slice strawberries into chunks so they get down into the blender blades. Add the juice of half a lemon. Add the stevia and blend until smooth. Add in ice cubes two at a time until your desired consistency is reached. Too much ice could make it watery so try it with 4-5 ice cubes to start, and then go from there. Pour into a tall glass and garnish with a fresh lemon wedge. You could also rim the glass with some lemon and a little stevia for a little extra sweet/sour!
Serving Size – 1 Fruit, ½ Lemon

YUMMY VANILLA ICED COFFEE
1 c. espresso strength coffee, cooled
1 TBSP milk
Few drops Vanilla Crème stevia
Sprinkle of spice, if desired (cinnamon, pumpkin, etc)
4-5 ice cubes

Blend in blender with crushed ice until frothy. Delicious!!!
Serving Size – 1 Milk

BLOODY MARY

1 medium sized tomato
Juice of ½ lemon
1 tsp fresh cilantro, minced
Stevia, to taste
1 clove garlic, minced
¼ tsp cumin
Salt/pepper, to taste
Tabasco, to taste

Combine all ingredients in a blender and puree until reaches desired consistency. Serve chilled or over ice.
Serving Size – 1 Vegetable, ½ Lemon

VANILLA HOT COCOA

8 oz. hot water
5 drops Chocolate stevia
2 drops Vanilla Creme stevia

Place 8oz of water in a coffee mug. Add stevia and mix.

CREAMY CAFE 'LATTE'

1 c. pure coffee
1 TBSP of milk
Vanilla Creme and Dark Chocolate stevia drops

Place hot coffee in a coffee mug. Add stevia and mix.
Serving Size – 1 Milk

PUMPKIN MOCHA WARM-UP
1 c. coffee
1 TBSP milk
½ tsp pumpkin pie spice (Check for sugars)
Dark chocolate or milk chocolate stevia, to taste

Place all items in a mug. Stir until desired consistency.
Serve.
Serving Size – 1 Milk

ORANGE DELIGHT
¾ c. crushed ice
1 orange
2 stalks celery
5 drops Valencia Orange flavored stevia

Mix in blender or juicer until smooth. Pour into glass and
serve.
Serving Size – 1 Fruit, 1 Vegetable

SUMMERTIME LEMONADE
1 c. water
Juice of 1 lemon
Regular stevia, to taste

Take 8oz of water and add the juice of ½ a lemon. Add
Stevia to taste.
Serving Size – 1 Lemon

ORANGE DREAM

¾ c. crushed ice
1 orange
5 drops Vanilla Creme flavored stevia

Mix in blender until smooth. Pour into glass and serve.
Serving Size – 1 Fruit

ENGLISH TOFFEE COFFEE

1 c. coffee
English Toffee stevia drops

Place coffee in a coffee mug. Add stevia and serve.
Serving Size – 1 Milk

FROZEN COFFEE

8oz coffee, cooled
1 TBSP milk
5 drops Vanilla Crème flavored stevia (could use other
flavors depending on your preference)
4–5 ice cubes

Combine all ingredients in a blender and blend until
desired consistency. Serve.
Serving Size – 1 Milk

Fish and Seafood (22)

ASPARAGUS WITH GARLIC SHRIMP

100 grams shrimp
Salt, to taste
Paprika, to taste
4 TBSP water
1 garlic clove, minced
¼ tsp crushed red pepper flakes
Juice of 1 lemon (split)
2 TBSP minced parsley
2 c. asparagus
Black pepper to taste

Shell the shrimp and sprinkle with salt and paprika, set aside. Mix the water, garlic and pepper flakes into a medium-sized skillet. When the garlic is just beginning to brown, add the shrimp and cook, stirring for about 1 minute, or until just done and firm to the touch. Stir in 1 TBSP of lemon juice and parsley. In a separate frying pan, place asparagus with about ¼ inch of water in the bottom. Use the rest of the alloted lemon juice along with enough black pepper to taste. Cook on high until desired texture is reached. Serve immediately.
Serving Size – 1 Protein, 1 Vegetable, 1 Lemon

BOILED SHRIMP

100 grams shrimp
2–3 c. water (enough to cover shrimp in pan)
¼ c. apple cider vinegar
2 TBSP seafood seasoning (Found under 'Sauces, Rubs, Dressings and Marinades section)

Add water, apple cider vinegar, seafood seasoning and shrimp to saucepan over medium–high heat. Let water come to a slow boil. When shrimp start to float, remove from heat and drain. Either serve hot or immediately place shrimp in ice water for 1 minute. Drain and serve immediately, or chill in refrigerator.
Serving Size – 1 protein

HOT WASABI WHITE FISH

100 grams white fish
1 TBSP dry mustard
1 TBSP water
½ – 1 tsp wasabi powder (adjust to the desired level of spice)
½ tsp ginger

In a small dish, combine dry mustard, wasabi powder and 1 TBSP of water to make a paste. Add more water if needed. Mix in the ginger. Add fish to the dish and coat. Let stand for 15–30 minutes. Grill 4–5 minutes until fish flakes. Or you can broil for 5–10 minutes depending on thickness of fish. Serve immediately.
Serving Size – 1 protein

CRAB CAKES

100 grams raw crab meat
1 Grissini (ground into powder)
1 tsp parsley
½ tsp tarragon
½ tsp paprika
½ tsp lemon juice
¼ tsp cayenne
¼ tsp white pepper
¼ tsp dry mustard
¼ tsp seafood seasoning (Found under 'Sauces, Rubs, Dressings and Marinades section)

Grind up Grissini into powder and place in a dish. You can grind up the Grissini by placing it into a sandwich bag, then use a rolling pin to crush breadstick or by using a coffee grinder. In a bowl, mix crab meat and all other ingredients. Mix well and form into little cakes. Then coat each side of cake with grissini powder. Brown in a non-stick skillet over medium heat for 3 minutes each side. Serve immediately.
Serving Size – 1 Protein, 1 Breadstick

CURRIED BROILED FISH

100 grams fish
1 sliced tomato
½ lemon
½ - 1 tsp curry seasoning
½ tsp garlic
½ tsp salt
½ tsp pepper

Preheat oven to 350. Place fish on a pan with a little water in the bottom. Squeeze 1/2 lemon over fish. Sprinkle fish with all spices. Place tomato slices on top of fish. Bake for 10-15 minutes until tomato starts to blacken and fish begins to flake.
Serving Size - 1 Protein, 1 Vegetable, ½ Lemon

NOW THAT'S GARLIC! SHRIMP

100 grams shrimp
4-6 cloves garlic, minced
1/2 c. water
1/2 tsp parsley
1/8 tsp dried thyme
1/8 tsp crushed red pepper
1 bay leaf

Heat nonstick pan over medium-high heat. Mix 1 TBSP of water with red pepper, minced garlic, and bay leaf. Add to pan. Cook for about one minute. Be sure not to burn the garlic. Add shrimp. Cook 3 minutes. Remove shrimp from pan. Add the remaining water, parsley, and thyme. Bring to a boil. Cook for 1-2 minutes until reduced by half. Return shrimp to pan & toss to coat. Discard bay leaf and serve.
Serving Size - 1 Protein

CREOLE FISH

100 grams white fish
1 chopped tomato
½ c. water
1 – 2 tsp Cajun seaonsing (Found under 'Sauces, Rubs, Dressings and Marinades section)

Heat pan over medium-high heat. Cut fish into 1 inch pieces. Place fish in a sandwich bag. Add cajun seasoning to coat. Pan fry coated fish in pan with water. Cook 3–4 minutes. Add more water as needed. Add chopped tomato & cook for another 5–10 minutes until tomatoes become tender and dish becomes more soupy.
Serving Size – 1 Protein, 1 Vegetable

RED SNAPPER WITH FENNEL

100 grams red snapper (or any white fish)
Fennel – cut into 1″ pieces
Juice of 1 lemon
2 tsp fresh ginger
1 tsp pepper
1 tsp salt

Place fish in shallow dish. Squeeze lemon juice in small bowl. Stir in ginger & pepper to make a sauce. Pour the sauce on the fish and refrigerate for 1–3 hours. Remove fish from the dish and place in glass baking dish. Cover with chopped fennel. Cover dish with aluminum foil and bake at 350 for 20–30 minutes or until fish flakes.
Serving Size – 1 Protein, 1 Vegetable, 1 Lemon

SPICY CILANTRO WHITEFISH

100 grams fish
Juice of 1/2 lemon
1/2 c. cilantro
3 cloves garlic, minced
1 TBSP sambal oelek
1 TBSP water (as needed)
½ tsp red pepper flakes
½ tsp paprika

Preheat oven to 400. In food processor, combine lemon juice, cilantro, garlic, sambal oelek, red pepper flakes and paprika. Start to pulse and add water as necessary until it reaches desired consistency. Place fish in baking dish or non-stick baking sheet. Brush on spice mix. Bake for 10–20 minutes, depending on thickness, until fish flakes.
Serving Size – 1 Protein, ½ Lemon

LEMON SHRIMP AND SPINACH

100 grams shrimp (peeled & deveined)
2 c. spinach
3 TBSP water
Juice of 1 lemon
4-5 cloves garlic, minced
Salt and pepper, to taste

Preheat non-stick skillet over medium heat. Add 3 TBSP of water, garlic, and shrimp. Cook 5 minutes or until shrimp just turns pink. Add water as necessary. Squeeze in juice of 1 lemon. Add spinach. Toss in salt & pepper. Cook uncovered until spinach wilt.
Serving Size – 1 Protein, 1 Vegetable, 1 Lemon

CAJUN SHRIMP KABOBS

100 grams shrimp
Juice of ½ lemon
Fresh parsley, chopped
1 TBSP Cajun seasoning (Found under 'Sauces, Rubs, Dressings and Marinades section)

Place shrimp in bowl & add 1 TBSP of Cajun Seasoning, toss to coat. Put shrimp on skewers (if using wood skewers, remember to soak in water for at least 20 minutes prior to use). You can also make kebobs with onion, tomato OR any other veggie allowed on protocol. Squeeze on lemon juice. Grill or broil until cooked through. Sprinkle with chopped parsley.
Serving Size – 1 Protein, ½ Lemon

STUFFED TOMATOES

100 grams shrimp
1 tomato (allowed amount)
Juice of ½ lemon
1 TBSP parsley
Salt/pepper to taste
Tabasco (optional)

Cook shrimp in water until thoroughly done. Chop shrimp into small pieces. In a small bowl, combine chopped shrimp, parsley, lemon juice, salt and pepper. Cover and refrigerate for 30 minutes – 1 hour. When ready to serve, cut off top of tomato. Scoop out inside of tomato with a spoon. Chop and combine inside of tomato with shrimp mix if desired. Fill tomato with shrimp mix and serve. Make extra for an easy lunch on the go.
Serving Size – 1 Protein, 1 Vegetable, ½ Lemon

CURRY SHRIMP

100 grams shrimp
1 c. onion, chopped
1-2 cloves garlic, minced
1/8 c. water
½ tsp. curry powder
¼ tsp. cumin
¼ tsp. turmeric
Salt and pepper to taste

Preheat pan over medium heat. Add onion & garlic with a little bit of water, 1-2 TBSP. Cook until translucent about 5-10 minutes. Add shrimp and seasonings to the onions and garlic. Mix & stir fry until cooked through, then serve.
Serving Size - 1 Protein, 1 Vegetable

LEMON PEPPER FISH

100 grams white fish
Juice of ½ lemon
3 cloves garlic, minced
½ tsp black pepper
¼ tsp salt
¼ tsp cumin powder
¼ tsp coriander
1/8 tsp tumeric

Place fish in a bowl. Add garlic, black pepper, salt, cumin, coriander & tumeric. Coat both sides. Cover & marinate at least 1 hour in the fridge. Preheat oven to 400. Place the fish in a non-stick baking dish and brush with the marinade. Bake 10-20 minutes depending on thickness, until fish easily flakes. Squeeze with lemon juice & serve.
Serving Size - 1 Protein, ½ Lemon

ROCK LOBSTER WITH ASPARAGUS

1 tsp salt
1 tsp paprika
1/8 tsp white pepper
1/8 tsp garlic powder
2 TBSP water
Juice of 1 lemon – divided
2 – 10 oz. thawed rock lobster tails (3oz of lobster = 1 protein serving)
1 c. asparagus

Split rock tails lengthwise with a large knife. Mix seasonings with lemon juice and water. Brush meat side of tail with marinade. Pre-heat grill and place rock tails meat side down and grill five to six minutes until well scored. Turn over lobster and cook another six minutes, brushing often with remaining marinade. Lobster is done when it is opaque and firm to the touch. Place asparagus in a pan with about ¼ inch water, juice from ½ lemon and pepper to taste. Cook on medium heat, and remove once the desired texture is reached. Serve immediately.
Serving Size – 1 Protein, 1 Vegetable, 1 Lemon

LEMON OREGANO WHITE FISH WITH ASAPARGUS

100 grams white fish
1 c. asparagus
Juice of 1 lemon
1 tsp oregano
1 tsp parsley
Salt and pepper, to taste

Preheat oven to 400F. Cut off ends of asparagus and discard. Take a large sheet of non-stick aluminum foil. In the center of this sheet, place asparagus spears and sprinkle with salt/pepper. Place fish on top of asparagus. In a small bowl, combine lemon juice, oregano and parsley, then pour over the fish. Fold up edges and completely seal packet on all sides. Bake 10-20 minutes, until fish flakes, then serve.
Serving Size - 1 Protein, 1 Vegetable, 1 Lemon

GARLIC SHRIMP

100 grams shrimp
1 c. diced tomatoes OR spinach
1/8 tsp garlic
1/8 tsp salt
1 c. water
Pepper to taste

Place all ingredients in a saucepan and boil for 5 minutes or until shrimp is done. Serve immediately.
Serving Size - 1 Protein, 1 Vegetable

YOURHCG.COM CIOPPINO

100 grams white fish
1 chopped tomato
2 c. water
3 cloves garlic, minced
1 tsp parsley
¼ tsp oregano
¼ tsp basil
1/8 tsp rosemary
Salt/pepper to taste
Tabasco

Combine parsley, oregano, basil, and rosemary in food processor and grind. Add seasonings and all other ingredients except for fish & Tabasco to pan.
Bring to a boil. Reduce heat, cover, and simmer for 30 minutes. Add fish and return to a boil. Reduce heat and cover and simmer for 5-15 minutes. Top with a few dashes of Tabasco just before serving.
Serving Size - 1 Protein, 1 Vegetable

FISH WITH A LEMON TWIST
100 grams whitefish
½ tsp ground ginger, divided
Juice of 1 lemon, divided
Salt/pepper to taste
2 c. cabbage, sliced
½ c. water

Mix together ¼ tsp ginger, juice of ½ lemon, salt and pepper. In a sandwich bag, marinate fish with ginger sauce for 1 hour. Bake on 350 for 10-20 minutes, depending on thickness, until fish flakes. In the mean time, preheat pan to medium-high heat. Add water, ¼ tsp of ginger, juice of ½ lemon, salt, pepper and cabbage to the pan. Stir fry until the cabbage reaches your desired consistency.
Serving Size – 1 Protein, 1 Vegetable, 1 Lemon

TERIYAKI FISH
100 grams whitefish
1 TBSP water
2 cloves garlic, minced
1 tsp ginger
Juice of ½ lemon

In a small bowl, add water, garlic, ginger and lemon. Add fish and cover with sauce. Marinate in fridge for 1 hour. Grill the fish until the fish flakes.
Serving Size – 1 Protein, ½ Lemon

SPICY SHRIMP STIR FRY

100 grams shrimp
2 cloves garlic, minced
1 c. asparagus
1 TBSP ginger
½ c. water

In a pan, add shrimp, garlic and ginger. Stir fry for 5 minutes adding water as needed. In the meantime, cut asparagus into 2 inch pieces. Remove shrimp from pan. Add aspargus with a little bit of water. Leave the ginger and garlic in the pan to add flavor to the asparagus. Cook asparagus for 3 minutes. Add shrimp to asparagus mixture, cook for 1 minute, then serve.
Serving Size – 1 Protein, 1 Vegetable

KUNG PAO SHRIMP

100 grams shrimp
1 c. chopped onion
1-2 tsp sambal oelek
Red pepper flakes (optional)

Marinade
1 part liquid aminos

Seasoning
Mix together in small bowl:
3 cloves garlic, minced
1 tsp curry seasoning
1-2 tsp fresh ginger root, minced

Sauce
Stir together in small bowl:
1/2 c. water
1-2 tsp liquid aminos

In small dish, combine marinade & shrimp. Marinate for 30 minutes in the fridge. On medium-high heat, cook shrimp until done. Add sambal oelek. Cook 1-3 additional minutes. Remove shrimp from pan and set aside. Add onion to pan and cook until tender. Add sauce mixture to pan. Cook for 3 minutes. Add the shrimp back to the pan. Stir and cook for an additional 3 minutes. Top with a few dashes of red pepper flakes.
Serving Size - 1 Protein, 1 Vegetable

Chicken (20)

BREADED CHICKEN 'TENDERS'
100 grams chicken breast
1 Grissini breadtick (ground into powder)
½ c. water
¼ tsp garlic powder
¼ tsp paprika
¼ tsp YourHCG.com Basic Seasoning (Found under 'Sauces, Rubs, Dressings and Marinades section)
¼ tsp cayenne
Salt/pepper to taste

Preheat pan over medium heat. In small dish, combine grissini powder, garlic powder, paprika, basic seasoning, cayenne, and salt/pepper. Add chicken to seasonings and fully coat. Add half of the water and chicken to pan. Cook for approx. 3–4 minutes each side depending on thickness of chicken, until done.
Serving Size – 1 Protein, 1 Breadstick

BAKED CAJUN CHICKEN
100 grams chicken breast
1 TBSP milk
½ tsp Your HCG.com Cajun seasoning (Found under 'Sauces, Rubs, Dressings and Marinades section)

Preheat oven to 350. In a small dish containing the milk, cover both sides of the chicken with milk. Put Cajun seasoning in a sandwich bag. Place chicken in bag, seal and shake. Bake chicken in an uncovered baking dish for 20–30 minutes until chicken is no longer pink, then serve.
Serving Size – 1 Protein, 1 Milk

RED HOT CHILE CHICKEN

100 grams chicken breast
1 TBSP red chile paste
1 TBSP apple cider vinegar
3 cloves garlic, minced
1 tsp oregano
1 tsp parsley
½ tsp cumin
½ tsp stevia
Salt
Crushed red pepper (optional)

In sandwich bag, add all ingredients except chicken. Mix
well. Add the chicken to the bag. Seal and shake until
coated. Place in fridge to marinate for 30 minutes – 1
hour. Cook chicken until done. Top with crushed red
pepper and serve.
Serving Size – 1 Protein

LEMON MUSTARD CHICKEN

100 grams chicken breast
Juice of 1/2 lemon
1 TBSP dry mustard
½ tsp black pepper
¼ tsp parsley
½ tsp oregano
¼ tsp cayenne pepper

In small bowl, mix all ingredients, except chicken. Spoon
mixture onto chicken. Flip over and coat other side. Broil
each side 5–10 mins or until no longer pink, then serve.
Serving Size – 1 Protein, ½ Lemon

KUNG PAO CHICKEN

100 grams chicken breast – cut into chunks
1 c. chopped onion
1-2 tsp sambal oelek
Red pepper flakes (optional)

Marinade
1 part liquid aminos

Seasoning
Mix together in small bowl:
3 cloves garlic, minced
1 tsp curry seasoning
1-2 tsp fresh ginger root, minced

Sauce
Stir together in small bowl:
1/2 c. water
1-2 tsp liquid aminos

In small dish, combine marinade & chicken. Marinate for 30 minutes in the fridge. On medium-high heat, cook chicken until done, browning on all sides. Add sambal oelek. Cook 1-3 additional minutes. Remove chicken from pan and set aside. Add onion to pan and cook until tender. Add sauce mixture to pan. Cook for 3 minutes. Add the chicken back to the pan. Stir and cook for an additional 3 minutes. Top with a few dashes of red pepper flakes.
Serving Size – 1 Protein, 1 Vegetable

ORANGE GINGER CHICKEN

100 grams chicken breast
2 c. cabbage, cut in strips
1/4 c. water
Juice of ½ lemon
1 orange, peeled – squeeze the juice and add the pulp to
sauce
½ tsp fresh ginger, slivered or grated
4 TBSP of Bragg's Liquid Aminos
Salt and pepper to taste

In a small bowl add all the ingredients except the chicken
and cabbage. Whisk together. Place in a small frying pan
and add chicken. Cook chicken until done. Remove chicken
and add the cabbage with about ¼ cup of water. Cook
cabbage until it's to your desired texture. Add chicken
into pan. I had my cabbage cut long so it almost reminded
me of lo mein.
Serving Size – 1 Protein, 1 Vegetable, 1 Fruit, ½ Lemon

SPICY FRIED CHICKEN

100 grams chicken breast
1 TBSP milk
1 Grissini breadstick
Sea salt
Pepper
Cayenne pepper to taste

Crush breadstick in food processor or put in a plastic bag
and crush with a rolling pin. Dip chicken in milk and coat
with the breadstick crumbs. Cook in a nonstick pan.
Season with salt, pepper and cayenne.
Serving Size – 1 Protein, 1 Milk, 1 Breadstick

CABBAGE WRAPS

2–3 big cabbage leaves
1 c. shredded cabbage
1/8 tsp garlic powder
1/8 tsp Chinese Five Spice
1 piece Melba Toast
100 grams cooked chopped chicken breast or shrimp

Steam big cabbage leaves for 5 minutes. Move leaves over to side of steamer to make room for shredded cabbage. Steam both for 5 minutes. Remove shredded cabbage and place in a mixing bowl. Add chopped chicken or shrimp and spices to bowl. Mix and then wrap in big cabbage leaves. Garnish with Melba toast.
Serving Size – 1 Protein, 1 Vegetable, 1 Melba toast

OVEN FRIED GARLIC CHICKEN

4 – 100 gram pieces of chicken breast (4 servings)
3 tsp crushed garlic cloves
2 TBSP water
Dash of salt
Dash of pepper
½ tsp oregano
½ tsp basil

Place the garlic and water in a bowl, mix well. Add salt, pepper and herbs to form a paste, adding more water if needed. Rub all over the chicken pieces. Lay the chicken pieces in a baking pan and bake on 425 for 30 minutes. Serve with approved vegetable.
Serving Size – 1 Protein

SHISH KABOBS

100 grams chicken breast or shrimp
Choice of ONE – either onion or tomato
Juice of 1 lemon
¼ tsp rosemary
¼ tsp thyme
¼ tsp cumin

Place chunks of meat choice and vegetable choice on a skewer. Season with herbs and lemon juice prior to grilling. Place on grill, rotating for 10 minutes. If using wooden skewers, soak for 20 minutes first.
Serving Size – 1 Protein, 1 Vegetable, 1 Lemon

GARLIC CHICKEN

4 – 100 gram chicken breast (4 servings)
4 c. onion, diced (4 servings)
3–5 cloves garlic – unpeeled & left whole
Juice of 2 lemons
Black pepper, to taste

Preheat oven to 350. In a non-stick pan, add the onion and cook over medium heat. Stir constantly until tender, about 5-10 minutes. Transfer onions to glass baking dish. Place chicken on top of the onions. Squeeze the chicken with lemon juice & sprinkle with pepper. Place garlic around and on the chicken. Cover tightly either with lid or aluminum foil. Cook for 30-45 minutes or until chicken is no longer pink, then serve.
Serving Size – 1 Protein, 1 Vegetable, ½ Lemon

BLACKENED CHICKEN SALAD

100 grams chicken breast
1 tsp paprika
½ tsp garlic powder
¼ tsp oregano
¼ tsp thyme
¼ tsp white pepper
¼ tsp black pepper
¼ tsp ground red pepper
Spinach or salad greens

Cover chicken with all the spices. Cook until no longer pink. Serve over spinach or salad greens of your choice.
Serving Size – 1 Protein, 1 Vegeteable

BONELESS HOT WINGS

100 grams chicken breast
¼ c. white vinegar
¼ c. water
1–2 TBSP cayenne pepper
1–2 TBSP chili powder
Red Pepper Flakes (optional)

In small bowl, mix vinegar, water, and cayenne pepper. Add chicken to marinade and refrigerate for 1–2 hours. Preheat oven to 350. Sprinkle chicken with chili powder and red pepper flakes. Bake 15–20 minutes, or until thoroughly cooked.
Serving Size – 1 Protein

LEMON ROSEMARY CHICKEN

100 grams chicken breast
Juice of ½ lemon
½ tsp rosemary
¼ tsp pepper
1–2 cloves garlic, minced

Heat a non-stick pan over medium-high heat. In small bowl, grate lemon peel. Add lemon juice, rosemary, pepper, and garlic. Toss in chicken. Place chicken in skillet. Cook 5 minutes brushing with remaining juice mixture. Turn over chicken and cook 5 more mins or until juices run clear, then serve.
Serving Size – 1 Protein, ½ Lemon

MELBA DELIGHT

1 Melba toast
100 grams chicken breast – sliced
1 tomato, sliced
Pinch of oregano
Pinch of salt

Cook chicken with salt and oregano. Serve with sliced tomatoes and Melba toast.
Serving Size – 1 Protein, 1 Vegetable, 1 Melba toast

CHICKEN & TOMATOES

100 grams chicken breast
1 tomato, pureed
1 c. water
½ tsp sage
½ tsp garlic powder
½ tsp salt
½ tsp pepper

Place chicken in a baking dish. In a small bowl, mix tomatoes, water, sage, garlic, salt, and pepper. Pour sauce over chicken. Bake in the oven at 375 for 45 minutes, then serve.
Serving Size – 1 Protein, 1 Vegetable

SPICY CHICKEN

100 grams chicken breast
¼ tsp chili powder
¼ tsp cayenne pepper
½ tsp paprika
1 tomato, chopped
2 TBSP apple cider vinegar
Juice of ½ lemon
¼ tsp garlic powder

Preheat oven to 350 degrees. Mix chili powder, cayenne pepper, and paprika in a small bowl. Spread liberally on both sides of chicken. Place in a small baking dish. In a separate bowl, add tomatoes, apple cider vinegar, lemon juice and garlic powder. Mix well. Then pour over the chicken. Cook for 25–30 minutes at 350 degrees.
Serving Size – 1 Protein, 1 Vegetable, ½ Lemon

TERIYAKI CHICKEN

100 grams chicken breast
1 TBSP water
2 cloves garlic, minced
1 tsp ginger
Juice of ½ lemon

In a small bowl, add water, garlic, ginger and lemon. Add chicken and cover with sauce. Marinate in fridge for 1 hour. Grill the chicken until no longer pink. Serve.
Serving Size – 1 Protein, ½ Lemon

CHICKEN & 'SALSA'

100 grams chicken breast
1 tomato, diced
3 cloves garlic, minced
1 tsp oregano
1 tsp basil
1 tsp parsley
¼ tsp chili powder
Salt and pepper, to taste

Preheat oven to 350. In a casserole dish, place ½ of the diced tomato on the bottom, then place chicken on top of tomato. In a small bowl, toss rest of the tomato with all spices and place on top of the chicken. Cover, cook for 45–60 minutes, or until chicken is no longer pink. Serve
Serving Size – 1 Protein, 1 Vegetable

SWEET N SPICY CHICKEN WRAPS

100 grams chicken breast
4 cabbage leaves, whole
1 small Gala apple, cored and chopped
2 TBSP of Braggs Liquid Amino Acids
1 TBSP Tabasco
1 TBSP dry mustard
2 cloves garlic, minced
2 TBSP of water
Pepper, to taste
1 tsp garlic powder

In one small skillet add 100 grams of chicken in saute pan with 2 TBSP of Braggs Liquid Aminos, black pepper, and garlic powder. Cook chicken until done, adding water to deglaze pan and keep chicken moist. While chicken is cooking take another large pan (I use a 8" pan with high sides so the cabbage leaves lay open and will not tear) add water bring to a boil. Add cabbage leaves one at a time just to cook until cabbage leaf is tender and plyable. (I also remove the hard veins of larger leafs). As they are done take out and set aside. Once the chicken is completely cooked remove chicken from the pan, let cool and cut up. Keep the juice from the cooked chicken, add the minced garlic, 1 TBSP of mustard and 2 TBSP of water. Bring to a boil and cook your apples in this mixture. Once the apples start cooking down and are tender, return the chopped chicken to the apples. Take your large steamed cabbage leafs and spoon in the mixture and roll into wraps, then serve.

Serving Size – 1 Protein, 1 Fruit, 1 Vegetable

Beef (10)

BLUSTERY DAY CHILI
100 grams London Broil or Round Roast, chopped
2 cloves garlic, minced
1 tomato, chopped
½ c. water
¼ tsp garlic powder
¼ tsp chili powder
1/8 tsp oregano
Cayenne pepper, to taste (optional)
Salt and pepper, to taste

Brown beef in small frying pan, add garlic. Stir in tomatoes and water. Add spices and simmer slowly until liquid is reduced, about 30 minutes, then serve.
Serving Size – 1 Protein, 1 Vegetable

MEATBALLS
100 grams ground London broil or Round Roast
1 Grissini breadstick (ground into powder)
1 TBSP of milk
1/8 tsp each of parsley, basil, oregano, garlic, salt and pepper

Preheat oven to 425. In bowl, combine all ingredients. Then form into 1" meatballs (makes about 6–7 meatballs). Place in a baking dish on non stick aluminum foil and cook for 10 minutes, turning ½ way through, serve.
Serving Size – 1 Protein, 1 Breadstick, 1 Milk

MINI MEATLOAF

100 grams ground London Broil or Round Roast
½ tsp milk
1 Grissini breadstick, ground to powder
2-3 cloves garlic, minced
½ tsp dry mustard
¼ tsp pepper
¼ tsp salt
¼ tsp sage
¼ tsp oregano
Salt and pepper to taste

Preheat oven to 350. In small bowl, add all ingredients and form into a small loaf. Place in glass dish, cover and bake 25-30 minutes or until beef is cooked. Uncover dish, and bake for 5-10 minutes. Serve immediately.
Serving Size - 1 Protein, 1 Breadstick, ½ Milk

HCG FRIENDLY FRENCH DIP

100 grams London broil or Round Roast, sliced
1 onion, sliced into rings
1 c. water
2 cloves garlic, minced
½ tsp thyme
½ tsp pepper

In a warm pan, add onions and garlic, cook for 5 minutes, until translucent. Add water, thyme and pepper. Reduce heat & simmer for an additional 5 minutes. Add beef and return to boil, then reduce heat and simmer for 5 more minutes. Serve steak & onions with au jus sauce (left over sauce in the pan).
Serving Size - 1 Protein, 1 Vegetable

MEAT IN TOMATO SAUCE

100 grams of any approved HCG meat
1 large tomato
¼ tsp garlic salt
¼ tsp Italian Seasoning (make sure it has 0 carbs)

Slice up your tomato and put it into a sauce pan. Saute on medium for about 5 minutes. While it is being heated, occasionally smash the tomatoes with a spoon. While cooking the tomatoes, cook the meat of your choice. When your tomatoes are heated and soft, they should have the consistency of thick spaghetti sauce (or whatever consistency you prefer). After the meat is properly cooked, mix it together with the tomatoes. Add in your spices, stir.
Serving Size – 1 Protein, 1 Vegetable

ROSEMARY GARLIC STEAK

100 grams London broil or Round Roast
1 TBSP apple cider vinegar
1 TBSP rosemary
1–2 cloves garlic, minced
½ tsp crushed red pepper

In small dish, add vinegar and steak, then coat. Sprinkle beef with rosemary, garlic and red pepper. Make sure the steak is covered. Marinate in the fridge for 2–4 hours. Grill until desired doneness. Serve.
Serving Size – 1 Protein

YOURHCG.COM CINNAMON BEEF

100 grams of London Broil or Round Roast

¼ tsp cinnamon

¼ tsp parsley flakes

¼ tsp black pepper

¼ tsp garlic powder

In a small bowl, add the cinnamon, parsley, black pepper and garlic powder in a bowl. Then take the beef and rub the seasoning all over. Place on a George Foreman grill and cook to your liking. Serve with HCG friendly onion rings, cabbage, or a nice green salad.

Serving Size – 1 Protein

HCG & FAMILY FRIENDLY ROAST

3 lb lean London broil or Round Roast, fat removed

6–8 large cloves garlic

1 tsp dry oregano

1 tsp sea salt

Fresh ground pepper

Water

1/6 head of cabbage OR 1 onion

Place all ingredients in the roaster, add water until it is about 1 1/2 inches deep, and bake for 15 minutes on 350. Optionally, add potatoes and carrots for the family and cabbage or onion for the HCG dieter. Continue baking an additional 45–60 minutes depending upon how done you like your roast. Slice off 3 oz. of lean roast for the HCG dieter. Serve with your approved vegetable.

Serving Size – 1 Protein, 1 Vegetable

BEEF AND CABBAGE STIR FRY

100 grams London broil or Round Roast, sliced into strips
2 c. cabbage, thinly sliced strips
4 TBSP water, divided
1 clove garlic, minced
½ tsp cumin
½ tsp coriander
¼ tsp salt
¼ tsp pepper

In a preheated pan, add cabbage and 2 TBSP water. Cook
for about 2-3 minutes. Remove cabbage and place on a
plate. Add beef, remaining water and all spices. Cook until
beef is to your preferred doneness. Add cabbage and stir-
fry for 2-3 minutes.
Serving Size - 1 Protein, 1 Vegetable

STEAK & TOMATOES

100 grams London broil or Round Roast
1 tomato, diced
3 cloves garlic, minced
1 tsp oregano
1 tsp basil
1 tsp parsley
¼ tsp chili powder
Salt and pepper, to taste

Preheat oven to 350. In a casserole dish, place ½ of the
diced tomato on the bottom, then place steak on top of
tomato. In a small bowl, toss rest of the tomato with all
spices and place on top of the steak. Cover, cook for 45-
60 minutes. Serve
Serving Size - 1 Protein, 1 Vegetable

Vegetables (15)

SOUTHERN STYLE GREENS
4 TBSP water
2 c. beet greens, chopped
Dash of garlic salt
Red pepper flakes

Bring water to a boil. Reduce heat, add greens and red pepper flakes. Saute a few minutes until tender. Sprinkle with garlic salt and serve.
Serving Size – 1 Vegetable

SAUTEED GARLIC GREENS
6 cloves garlic, sliced
16 c. stemmed and rougly chopped chard (8 servings)
Red pepper flakes, to taste
1 TBSP kosher salt

Cook garlic in a preheated pan for about 2–3 minutes, or until translucent. Transfer to a small bowl and set aside. Cook greens, red pepper flakes and salt in the same skillet you used for the garlic, with water. Turn greens until wilted enough to fit in pan. Cook 7–10 minutes, turning frequently. Drain greens, then return to pan and toss with cooked garlic. Refrigerate leftover greens in an airtight container for up to 3 days.
Serving Size – 1 Vegetable

SALSA

1 tomato
Juice of ½ lemon
1/8 tsp chili powder
3 drops Clear stevia
1 tsp fresh cilantro, chopped
1/8 tsp garlic powder
1/8 c. Vinaigrette dressing (Found under 'Sauces, Rubs, Dressings and Marinades section)

Chop or puree tomato. Combine dressing, lemon juice, spices and stevia. Toss in tomato and refrigerate for at least 1 hour.
Serving Size - 1 Vegetable, ½ Lemon

GOOD FOR YOU ONION RINGS

1 c. onions, sliced
1 Melba toast or Grissini breadstick
1 TBSP milk
¼ tsp cayenne pepper
¼ tsp salt
¼ tsp pepper

Preheat oven to 450. In a small bowl, add milk, cayenne pepper, salt, and pepper. Mix to make a batter. Grind grissini in food processor until it's powder, then put the breadstick in a separate small bowl. Place rings in the batter bowl and toss to coat fully. Let the rings sit in the batter for 2-3 minutes, then toss again. Dip each ring into the grissini powder by hand. Do this one slice at a time. Place on a cookie sheet lined with non-stick aluminum foil. Cook 6-7 minutes, then flip, cooking both sides.
Serving Size - 1 Vegetable, 1 Breadstick, 1 Milk

ROASTED GARLIC ASPARAGUS

2 c. asparagus
1–2 cloves garlic, minced
¼ tsp oregano
Black pepper (to taste)

Preheat oven to 400. Trim asparagus. Spread the spears on a sheet of non-stick aluminum foil. Add the seasonings. Wrap all ends of the foil up tightly to make a sealed 'pocket'. Roast 15–20 minutes, then serve.
Serving Size – 1 Vegetable

GRILLED ONIONS

1 c. onions, sliced
½ tsp salt
½ tsp garlic powder
¼ c. water

In a frying pan, add water and bring to a light boil. Add onions and seasonings. Stir until cooked to your desired tenderness. Serve.
Serving size – 1 Vegetable

TANGY CRUNCHY CABBAGE

2 c. cabbage, shredded
1/8 c. water
¼ c. apple cider vinegar
Salt and pepper to taste

Place all ingredients in a frying pan. Stir contantly until cabbage is at your desired consistency, then serve.
Serving Size – 1 Vegetable

CUCUMBER DILL SALAD

2 c. cucumbers, thinly sliced
1 TBSP vinegar (to taste)
1 tsp dill
½ tsp zsweet (as needed)
Black pepper

Combine all ingredients except cucumber & mix well. Toss in cucumbers. Cover & refrigerate. This tastes best if you wait at least one hour before serving.
Serving Size – 1 Vegetable

CUCUMBER WITH MINT SALAD

2 c. cucumber, sliced or diced
1 TBSP vinegar (vary to taste – as I usually add about 3 TBSP)
1 tsp black pepper
1 tsp garlic, minced
1 tsp dried mint

Toss & mix all ingredients. Cover. Refrigerate for at least 1 hour. Toss again before serving.
Serving Size – 1 Vegetable

LEMON GINGER ASPARAGUS

1 c. asparagus
½ c. water
½ TBSP fresh ginger root, minced
3 cloves garlic, minced
Lemon zest
Black pepper

Cut off ends of asparagus spears & discard. Snap spears into 2-3 pieces. Add garlic & ginger to the pan and saute for 2-3 minutes. Add asparagus & water. Bring to a boil for 5 minutes. Remove asparagus and top with lemon zest & pepper, then serve.
Serving Size – 1 Vegetable

CABBAGE

2 c. cabbage
Juice of ½ lemon
½ tsp mustard seed
½ tsp garlic powder
Salt & pepper to taste

Place cabbage leaves in a steamer. Steam for about 5-10 minutes until they reach your desired texture. In a bowl, combine lemon juice, mustard, and garlic powder. Place cabbage in the bowl, and then lightly toss until well coated. Sprinkle the cabbage with salt & pepper, and then serve.
Serving Size – 1 Vegetable, ½ Lemon

PICKLES

1 cucumber, sliced
4 cloves garlic, minced
¼ c. apple cider vinegar (you can add more if you like it tangy)
Juice of 1 lemon
¼ tsp salt

In a canning jar, add all ingredients except cucumber. Mix well. Add cucumber. Mix so the cucumbers don't stick together. Refrigerate overnight, and serve.
Serving Size – 1 Vegetable, 1 Lemon

SPICY CUCUMBERS

1 cucumber, sliced
1 TBSP apple cider vinegar
1/8 tsp garlic powder
1/8 tsp cayenne

In a bowl, add all ingredients. Cover and marinate for 1-2 hours, then serve.
Serving Size – 1 Vegetable

GARLIC SPINACH CHIPS

2 c. spinach
¼ tsp salt
½ tsp garlic powder
May also use basil, pepper, rosemary, thyme, etc.

Preheat oven to 350. On a baking sheet with parchment paper, spread spinach out in a single layer. Sprinkle with seasonings. Bake for 7-10 minutes, until they are crispy. Remove from oven and remove carefully from parchment paper. Serve.
Serving Size - 1 Vegetable

BBQ ONIONS

1 onion
Juice of ½ lemon
½ tsp garlic powder
½ tsp chili powder

Heat BBQ grill while preparing onion. In a small bowl, mix lemon juice, garlic powder and chili powder. Cut onion in 2 halves, and place each half onto a piece of foil. The foil should be large enough to wrap around onion completely. Pour half of the seasoning mix on each onion. Wrap foil around onion, so no juices can escape. BBQ onion on the grill for 5-10 minutes, until you reach desired consistency. This is great served with Teriyaki Chicken or Meatballs.
Serving Size - 1 Vegetable, ½ Lemon

Soups (15)

CINNAMON CURRY BEEF SOUP
100 grams London Broil, cooked & cubed
1 c. onion, diced
2 c. water
3 cloves garlic, minced
½ tsp curry powder
¼ tsp cinnamon
Salt and black pepper, to taste

In saucepan, combine all ingredients. Bring to a boil.
Reduce heat, cover and simmer for 45 minutes.
Serving Size – 1 Protein, 1 Vegetable

CHICKEN RADISH SOUP
1 c. radishes, sliced
100 grams chicken breast, cooked & cubed
1–2 cloves garlic, minced
2 c. water (vary liquid amount depending on amt of soup
wanted)
Salt, to taste
Pepper, to taste

Combine all ingredients in saucepan. Bring to a boil.
Reduce heat and simmer 10–15 minutes. Serve
immediately.
Serving Size – 1 Protein, 1 Vegetable

CREAM OF CHICKEN SOUP

100 grams chicken breast, cooked
2 c. celery, chopped
1 – 2 c. water
3 cloves garlic, minced
½ tsp parsley
½ tsp basil
½ tsp white pepper
Salt, to taste

Place all ingredients into a saucepan and bring to a boil.
Reduce heat to simmer, cover and cook for 30 minutes. In
a blender or food processor, combine all ingredients and
pulse until it reaches a soupy texture. Serve.
Serving Size – 1 Protein, 1 Vegetable

LEMON CHICKEN SOUP

100 grams chicken breast, diced
2 c. spinach, chopped
2–3 c. water
Juice of 1 lemon
1 tsp thyme
1 tsp oregano
Sea salt, to taste
Ground white pepper, to taste

Combine all ingredients. Bring to a boil, simmer for 20
minutes and serve.
Serving Size – 1 Protein, 1 Vegetable, 1 Lemon

ITALIAN BEEF SOUP

100 grams ground London Broil or Round Roast
1 large tomato, chopped
1–2 c. water (adjust to how 'soupy' you'd like it)
1 clove garlic, minced
1/8 tsp oregano
1/8 tsp white pepper
1/8 tsp Italian Seasoing
Sea salt, to taste

Cook beef thoroughly with either a George Foreman grill or in a pan with 1 TBSP water. Combine chopped tomato, water, minced garlic, spices and beef. Bring to a boil. Reduce heat to low and simmer for 30 minutes before serving.
Serving Size – 1 Protein, 1 Vegetable

HOT & SOUR SHRIMP SOUP

100 grams cooked shrimp (may use chicken instead)
2 c. bok choy OR 1c. asparagus
2 c. water
1 tsp sambal oelek
½ tsp white pepper
¼ tsp ginger
Crushed red pepper

In saucepan, combine water, ginger, sambal oelek and white pepper. Bring to a boil. Reduce heat and simmer for 2–3 minutes. Add shrimp or chicken. Return to a boil. Add the vegetable of choice, cover, and simmer for 3 minutes. Sprinkle with crushed red pepper and serve.
Serving Size – 1 Protein, 1 Vegetable

YOUR HCG CHICKEN BROTH

6 – 100 gram pieces of chicken breast (6 servings)
8 c. water
1 tsp garlic powder
1 tsp poultry seasoning (Found under 'Sauces, Rubs, Dressings and Marinades section)
1 tsp black pepper
3 tsp sea salt

Combine ingredients in soup pot and cook until chicken is done. Remove chicken and refrigerate or freeze to use at a later time (I like to save it to put on salads). Also freeze bouillon base for future recipes. Put 2 cups in a medium size container to make soups or 4 tablespoons in a small container to saute.
Serving Size – 1 Protein

FRENCH ONION SOUP

2 c. Your HCG Chicken Broth (below)
1 sweet onion, sliced

Combine boullion base along with the sliced onion. Place in a pan and cook over medium heat until onions are tender. Serve.
Serving Size – 1 Vegetable

CHICKEN (FORGO THE) TORTILLA SOUP

1 c. tomatoes, chopped

1 TBSP garlic, minced

1 TBSP cumin

¼ tsp red repper

Pinch of sea salt

½ tsp black pepper

2 TBSP liquid aminos

½ c. water

4 TBSP fresh cilantro

100 grams chicken breast, cooked & shredded

1 Melba toast or Grissini breadstick

Preheat pot over medium–high heat. Blanch tomatoes in boiling water, drain and drench in cold water, peel skins and crush in the pot with your fingers or fork. Add minced garlic, cumin, chili powder, cayenne, red pepper, salt and black pepper. Continue to crush the tomatoes to your desired consistency with a fork. Add 1–2 TBSP liquid aminos (you don't have to be precise. I just throw a bit in for good measure). Add 1/4–1/2 cup water. Add 2 of the 4 tbsp of fresh chopped cilantro. Bring to low boil. Reduce heat to a simmer and add chicken. Simmer for 10 minutes more. Stir in last bit of cilantro before serving. Serve with your Grissini breadstick on the side or break into 1″ pieces on top like traditional tortilla soup.

Serving Size – 1 Protein, 1 Vegetable, 1 Breadstick

HOT & SPICY WHITE CHILI

100 grams cooked chicken breast, shredded
1 c. diced onion OR 1 large tomato
1-4 c. water (depending on how soupy you want it)
2 cloves garlic, minced
½ tsp. chili powder
1/8 tsp. garlic powder
½ tsp cumin
¼ tsp oregano
¼ tsp red pepper flakes
1/8 tsp ground cloves
3 -4 shakes sugar free hot sauce to taste

Add all ingredients except for tabasco/hot sauce into a crock pot. Cook on high for 4 hours or low for 6 hours. Add tabasco or hot sauce right before serving.
Serving Size - 1 Protein, 1 Vegetable

MEATBALL SOUP

1 serving of meatballs (recipe in Beef Recipe Section)
2 c. water
2 c. cabbage or bok choy
¼ tsp each of parsley, basil, oregano, garlic, salt & pepper

In a pan, bring water to a boil. Add meatballs, vegetable and seasonings to water. Cover and simmer for 30 minutes. Serve.
Serving Size - 1 Protein, 1 Vegetable, 1 Breadstick, 1 Milk

YOURHCG.COM STEW

100 grams London Broil or Round Roast, chopped
¼ tsp salt
1/8 tsp pepper
1/8 tsp thyme
1/8 tsp marjoram
1/8 tsp rosemary
1/8 tsp basil
1/8 tsp sage
1 tomato, chopped
2 TBSP apple cider vinegar

Saute tomato in apple cider vinegar for about 5-7 minutes.
Add meat and cook until done. Add the rest of the spices
along with 1 cup of water. Bring to a boil, then reduce heat
and simmer for 45 minutes.
Serving Size - 1 Protein, 1 Vegetable

TOMATO SOUP

2 c. Your HCG Chicken Broth
1 c. tomato, chopped
4 basil leaves, sliced
2 cloves garlic, minced
¼ tsp oregano
¼ tsp parsley
1/8 tsp marjoram
Salt & pepper to taste

Place all ingredients into a sauce pan and cook over
medium-high heat. Warm until boiling. Reduce heat, and
allow to simmer for 20-30 minutes Place contents of sauce
pan into a blender, blend until it reaches desired.
Serving Size - 1 Vegetable

CHICKEN 'NOODLE' SOUP

100 grams chicken breast
2 c. water
2 c. sliced cabbage (slice into long, thin strips like noodles)
2 cloves garlic, minced
¼ tsp thyme
¼ tsp rosemary
¼ tsp basil
¼ tsp parsley
Salt & pepper to taste

Cook chicken and spices in a pan with a little water. In a separate pan, bring water to a boil. When chicken is done, place chicken and cabbage in boiling water. Reduce heat, and simmer for 30 minutes. You may add more water as needed.
Serving Size – 1 Protein, 1 Vegetable

SPICY SHRIMP & CABBAGE SOUP

100 grams shrimp
2 c. cabbage
2 c. water
2 cloves garlic, minced
1 bay leaf
½ tsp chili powder
¼ tsp paprika

In a saucepan, add water, shrimp, cabbage and spices. Bring to a boil. Once boiling, reduce heat and allow to simmer for 30 minutes. Remove bay leaf and serve
Serving Size – 1 Protein, 1 Vegetable

Salads (15)

CUCUMBER SALAD
2 c. cucumber, thinly sliced
1 TBSP white vinegar (to taste)
1 tsp dill
Black pepper (to taste)

Combine all ingredients except cucumber. Mix well. Toss
in the cucumbers. Cover & refrigerate for at least 1 hour.
Serving Size – 1 Vegetable

THAI CUCUMBER BEEF SALAD
100 grams London broil or Round Roast
1 tsp sambal oelek or red pepper flakes
2–3 cloves garlic, minced
¼ tsp ground white pepper
2–3 TBSP water
1 cucumber, chopped
Juice of 1/2 lemon
Chopped cilantro

Peel, seed, and slice cucumber. In small dish, add
cucumber, juice of 1/2 lemon, and chopped cilantro. Mix.
Marinate in the fridge while preparing the rest of the dish.
Slice steak into very thin slices. In small bowl, place steak,
sambal oelek, garlic, and white pepper. Be sure to coat
steak well. Place steak in pan with water. Stir fry for 2–5
minutes depending on how you like your steak cooked.
Serve immediately while hot over cold cucumbers.
Serving Size – 1 Protein, 1 Vegetable, ½ Lemon

CUCUMBER SHRIMP SALAD

1 c. cucumber, diced
100 grams shrimp, cooked & diced
White vinegar (to taste)
Juice of ½ lemon
Sugar–free hot sauce (to taste)

Place all the ingredients in a bowl and toss.
Serving Size – 1 Protein, 1 Vegetable, ½ Lemon

SPICY CRAB CUCUMBER SALAD

100 grams crab,shredded
1 c. cucumber
1 TBSP water
½ – 1 TBSP dry mustard
½ – 1 tsp wasabi powder

Peel, seed and dice cucumber. Combine water, dry
mustard and wasabi powder. Mix well, then add remaining
ingredients, toss & serve.
Serving Size – 1 Protein, 1 Vegetable

SHRIMP SALAD WITH VINAIGRETTE DRESSING

2 c. raw spinach
100 grams shrimp, grilled
Vinaigrette Dressing (Found under 'Sauces, Rubs,
Dressings and Marinades section)
1 piece Melba toast or 1 Grissini Breadstick

Grill shrimp. Arrange spinach on plate and add shrimp.
Spray or spoon on Vinaigrette Dressing. Serve with Melba
toast or Grissini breadstick.
Serving Size – 1 Protein, 1 Vegetable, 1 Breadstick

CRUNCHY ASIAN SALAD

2 c. romaine lettuce or spinach
1 orange, chopped
100 grams chicken breast
¼ tsp Chinese 5 spice
1/8 tsp garlic salt
1 packet stevia
1 piece of Melba Toast
Citrus Dressing (Found under 'Sauces, Rubs, Dressings and Marinades section)

Cook and chop chicken. Toss lettuce, orange, and chicken with Chinese Five Spice, garlic salt and stevia. Break Melba toast into small pieces, like croutons. Spray or spoon on Citrus Dressing.
Serving Size – 1 Protein, 1 Vegetable, 1 Fruit, 1 Melba Toast

YOURHCG.COM TACO SALAD

2 c. romaine lettuce
100 grams London Broil or Round Roast (can also use chicken breast)
¼ c. water
¼ tsp garlic powder
¼ tsp chili powder
¼ tsp cayenne
1 onion flavored Melba Toasts

Brown beef or chicken with seasonings. Drain well. Top lettuce with ground beef mixture. Sprinkle with ground melba toast.
Serving Size – 1 Protein, 1 Vegetable, 1 Melba toast

YOURHCG.COM CHOPPED CHICKEN SALAD

100 grams chicken breast, chopped
½ c. water
2 c. cabbage, chopped
Salt and pepper, to taste
1 apple, chopped
1 Melba toast or Grissini breadstick

Cook chicken along in ½ c. of water. You can boil the chicken and use the water that's left over as broth for this same meal. Pour chicken over bed of cabbage and let the cabbage absorb the water. Sprinkle with salt and pepper. Add apple chunks and mix the salad together. You may use one of the HCG friendly dressings with this salad as well, if the broth doesn't work for you.
Serving Size – 1 Protein, 1 Vegetable, 1 Fruit, 1 Breadstick

LEMON CHICKEN SALAD

2 c. raw spinach or romaine lettuce
1 apple, chopped
100 grams chicken breast (Use Lemon Rosemary Chicken recipe)
Your favorite hCG dressing (Found under 'Sauces, Rubs, Dressings and Marinades section)

Cook and chop chicken. Arrange spinach or lettuce on plate, sprinkle with chopped apple and chopped chicken. Spray or spoon on dressing.
Serving Size – 1 Protein, 1 Vegetable, 1 Fruit, ½ Lemon

APPLE COLESLAW

2 c. cabbage, sliced
1 apple, peeled and cut into chunks
¼ c. white vinegar
½ c. water
1 tsp. salt
Juice of ½ lemon
Stevia to taste

Place all ingredients in a bowl. Mix and chill before serving.
Serving Size – 1 Vegetable, 1 Fruit, ½ Lemon

CHICKEN CURRY SALAD

100 grams chicken breast
1 apple, diced
2 c. lettuce
¼ c. water
Juice of ½ lemon
¼ tsp garlic powder
¼ tsp curry powder
1/8 tsp cayenne pepper
1/8 tsp cinnamon
1/8 tsp turmeric

In a pan, over medium heat, add chicken, water, and spices to pan. Cook until chicken is done. Arrange lettuce and apples on a plate. Top with chicken and serve, using some of the leftover juice from the chicken as a dressing, if desired.
Serving Size – 1 Protein, 1 Vegetable, 1 Fruit, ½ Lemon

CHICKEN STRAWBERRY SALAD

2 c. lettuce
100 grams chicken, cooked
10 medium strawberries, sliced
YourHCG.com Vinaigrette Dressing (Found under 'Sauces, Rubs, Dressings and Marinades section)

Arrange lettuce on a plate. Top with chicken and strawberries. Add vinaigrette dressing and serve.
Serving Size – 1 Protein, 1 Vegetable, 1 Fruit

MELBA TOAST CROUTONS

1 Melba toast
1/8 tsp garlic powder
1/8 tsp paprika
Juice of ½ lemon
Salt & pepper to taste

Preheat oven to 350. In a sandwich bag, add all ingredients. Shake until well covered. Empty Melba toast on to a cookie sheet, laying flat. Bake for 5 minutes. Serve on salad.
Serving Size – 1 Melba toast, ½ Lemon

TILAPIA SALAD

2 c. lettuce
1 apple, seeded and diced
100 grams tilapia
Juice of ½ lemon
1 tsp apple cider vinegar

Place lettuce on plate and top with apple and cooked
tilapia. Sprinkle with lemon juice and apple cider vinegar.
Serving Size – 1 Protein, 1 Vegetable, 1 Fruit

YOUR HCG SPICY BEEF SALAD

100 grams London broil or Round Roast, sliced
1 tsp chili powder
1 tsp paprika
1 tsp garlic powder
¼ c. water
Juice of 1 lemon
2 c. lettuce
1 orange

In a frying pan, add water. Bring to slight boil, and then
add beef and seasonings. Cook until done, medium to well
done. On a plate, arrange lettuce and top with orange.
Then pour contents of frying pan onto the plate and serve.
Serving Size – 1 Protein, 1 Vegetable, 1 Fruit, 1 Lemon

Protein Shake Recipes (10)

**Protein shakes were not on the original protocol, use at your own risk. For best results, use the Your HCG protein replacement shakes 3–4 times per week. Shakes can be purchased by visiting www.yourhcg.com/purchase.

VANILLA SHAKE

1 c. water
1 scoop Your HCG Vanilla Whey Protein Shake

Blend and enjoy. May also add Vanilla Creme stevia drops for a more vanilla flavor OR add your favorite flavored stevia drops.
Serving Size – 1 Protein

STRAWBERRY SHAKE

1 c. water
1 scoop Your HCG Vanilla Whey Protein Shake
Handful of frozen strawberries

Blend and enjoy.
Serving Size – 1 Protein, 1 Fruit

ORANGE VANILLA SHAKE

1 c. water
1 scoop Your HCG Vanilla Whey Protein Shake
1 orange

Blend and enjoy.
Serving Size – 1 Protein, 1 Fruit

CHOCOLATE SHAKE

1 c. water
1 scoop Your HCG Chocolate Whey Protein Shake
2 TBSP defatted cocoa (found at health food stores)

Blend and enjoy. May also add flavored stevia drops for a more "chocolate" taste.
Serving Size – 1 Protein

CHOCOLATE STRAWBERRY SHAKE

1 c. water
1 scoop Your HCG Chocolate Whey Protein Shake
Handful of frozen strawberries
2 TBSP defatted cocoa (found at health food stores)

Blend and enjoy. May also add flavored stevia drops for a more "chocolate" taste.
Serving Size – 1 Protein, 1 Vegetable

CINNAMON SURPRISE

1 c. water
1 scoop Your HCG Vanilla Protein Shake
¼ tsp cinnamon
Ice if needed

Blend and enjoy.
Serving Size – 1 Protein

VANILLA COFFEE SHAKE
1 c. water
1 scoop Your HCG Vanilla or Chocolate Protein Shake
4 oz coffee
Ice if needed

Blend all ingredients together and enjoy.
Serving Size – 1 Protein

APPLE PIE SHAKE
1 c. water
1 scoop Your HCG Vanilla Protein Shake
1 apple, sliced to blend easily
¼ tsp cinnamon
¼ tsp nutmeg
Ice if needed

Blend and enjoy.
Serving Size – 1 Protein, 1 Fruit

TROPICAL SURPRISE SHAKE
1 c. water
1 scoop Your HCG Strawberry Protein Shake
1 orange
Ice if needed

Blend and enjoy.
Serving Size – 1 Protein, 1 Fruit

KICKSTART YOUR DAY SHAKE

1 c. water
1 scoop Your HCG Vanilla Protein Shake
1 apple
2 c. spinach
Ice if needed

Place all ingredients in a blender. Blend until your desired consistency is reached and enjoy.
Serving Size – 1 Protein, 1 Vegetable, 1 Fruit

Desserts and Fruits (10)

CINNAMON APPLESAUCE

5 apples (5 servings)
Juice of ½ lemon
½ c. water
1 packet stevia
½ tsp cinnamon

Peel, core and chop apples. Cook apples with water in a crock pot on low for 2 hours. When cooled, puree apples in blender while adding stevia and cinnamon. Divide into 5 equal portions. Refrigerate for up to 3 days.
Serving Size – 1 Fruit, ½ Lemon

CINNAMON SPICED GRAPEFRUIT

1/2 grapefruit
¼ tsp cinnamon
1–2 packets stevia
2 TBSP water

Using a serrated edge knife, cut grapefruit in half as normally would and place on a microwave safe plate. Cut around center core and rind. Place cinnamon, stevia and water in a bowl to make a paste. Pour sauce over grapefruit. Heat in microwave on high for 2 minutes.
Serving Size – 1 Fruit

YOURHCG.COM FRIENDLY APPLE COBBLER

1 apple, sliced
1/8 tsp cinnamon
1 packet stevia
1 TBSP milk

Toss the above ingredients and arrange on a microwave safe plate.

Topping:
1 Melba Toast
Cinnamon
¼ packet stevia

Sprinkle apples with crumbled Melba Toast rounds, cinnamon and 1/4 packet stevia. Heat in microwave for 2 minutes.
Serving Size – 1 Fruit, 1 Milk, 1 Melba Toast

STRAWBERRY SORBET

Handful of strawberries
Juice of 1 lemon
Stevia (as needed)
Water (if needed)

Freeze fresh strawberries about 1 hour. Blend strawberries, lemon juice & stevia in blender until very well blended. You can serve immediately or place in freezer to allow it to firm up even further.
Serving Size – 1 Fruit, 1 Lemon

BROILED CINNAMON GRAPEFRUIT
1/2 grapefruit
Cinnamon to taste (optional)

Take a grapefruit spoon and go around the inside peel of the grapefruit so that it cuts out the grapefruit from the peel. Separate the sections and place in a bowl. Sprinkle with cinnamon. Toss, then place back into grapefruit peel. Broil for about 3-5 minutes.
Serving Size - 1 Fruit

APPLESAUCE
1 apple, diced
3 TBSP water
Cinnamon (optional)

Peel, core, and dice apple. Place diced apple in mini-crockpot, add water. Sprinkle with cinnamon. Cook on low for two hours. When finished, place in blender to reach desired consistency. Serve warm or refrigerate and serve cold.
Serving Size - 1 Fruit

WARM CINNAMON APPLE
1 apple
Cinnamon to taste
Stevia to taste

Cut one apple in half and sprinkle enough cinnamon on the apple to completely cover the exposed tops. Place them on a plate and microwave for 2-3 minutes.
Serving Size - 1 Fruit

VANILLA STRAWBERRY DESSERT

Handful of strawberries
5 drops Vanilla Crème stevia
8–10 drops Chocolate or Chocolate Raspberry stevia
1 TBSP milk

Mix milk, Vanilla Crème stevia, and Chocolate stevia in a bowl. Mix in sliced strawberries and enjoy.
Serving Size – 1 Fruit, 1 Milk

YOURHCG.COM FRIENDLY 'PIE'

1 apple OR handful of strawberries
¼ tsp cinnamon
Few drops of Vanilla Crème stevia

Cut apples or strawberries into slices. Place in a saucepan on medium heat and sprinkle with cinnamon. Add a little water to the pan and simmer until fruit is soft. Then add a few drops of Vanilla Crème stevia.
Serving Size – 1 Fruit

STRAWBERRY SHORTCAKE

1 piece Melba toast
5 drops Vanilla Crème stevia
10 medium strawberries, sliced
1 TBSP milk

In a bowl crush, crush Melba toast in the bottom. Top with strawberries, milk and stevia. Serve.
Serving Size – 1 Fruit, 1 Melba toast, 1 Milk

Sauces, Rubs, Dressings and Marinades (15)

YOURHCG.COM BASIC SEASONING
** This seasoning is great for beef, chicken and seafood.
1 TBSP garlic powder
2 TBSP dried sage leaves, crumbled
2 TBSP dried parsley leaves
2 TBSP dried thyme leaves
2 TBSP rosemary
2 TBSP white pepper

Combine all of the ingredients in a bowl. Put in container with a tight fitting lid and store away from heat and light. Shake or stir to re-blend before each use.

INDIAN CURRY SEASONING
1 TBSP tumeric
1 TBSP coriander
2 tsp paprika
1 tsp pepper
1 tsp cumin
1 tsp ginger
½ tsp cloves
½ tsp cayenne

Mix and store in an airtight container.

SEAFOOD SEASONING

1 TBSP ground bay leaves

1 ½ tsp dry mustard

1 ½ tsp black pepper

¾ tsp ground nutmeg

½ tsp ground cloves

½ tsp ground ginger

½ tsp paprika

½ tsp red pepper

¼ tsp ground cardomom

¼ tsp ground mace

Mix all ingredients and store in an airtight container.

HCG FRIENDLY SHAKE N BAKE

¼ tsp coriander

¼ tsp cumin

¼ tsp thyme

¼ tsp red pepper flakes

1/8 tsp oregano

1/8 tsp paprika

1/8 tsp black pepper

1/8 tsp salt

Place all ingredients in a food processor or coffee grinder. Grind to a powder. Store in an air-tight container.

MARINARA SAUCE

1 tomato
3 c. water
1 tsp oregano
1 tsp basil
2 TBSP parsley
1 clove garlic, minced
1 tsp salt
¼ tsp pepper

Place diced tomato in a sauce pan. If you want chunky sauce, crush tomato with your hand in a sauce pan. If you prefer smoother sauce, puree tomato in blender then add to the pan. Add all spices. Bring to a slight boil, then immediately reduce heat to low, cover & simmer for 15 minutes, stirring often. Turn heat up to medium. Cook 5–10 more minutes stirring constantly. While cooking, start adding water 1T of water at a time until it reaches your desired consistency.
Serving Size – 1 Vegetable

CARIBBEAN CHICKEN RUB

1 TBSP parsley

1 tsp cumin

1 tsp chili powder

½ tsp black pepper

½ tsp allspice

¼ tsp cinnamon

This amount makes enough for 2 servings of chicken (possibly even more depending on how much seasoning you like) so you can shake both of them up in the ziplock, cook both, and then refrigerate the extra chicken.

BBQ RUB

2 TBSP paprika

1 TBSP ground cumin

1 TBSP black pepper

1 TBSP chili powder

Mix; store in air-tight container.

CAJUN SEASONING

1 TBSP chili powder

1 TBSP Hungarian paprika

1 tsp garlic powder

½ tsp dried oregano

½ tsp dried thyme

½ tsp cayenne pepper

½ tsp freshly ground pepper

Combine & store in airtight container.

GREEK SEASONING MIX

2 tsp oregano

1 ½ tsp garlic powder

1 tsp salt

1 tsp black pepper

1 tsp parsley

1 tsp basil

1 tsp cumin

½ tsp cinnamon

½ tsp nutmeg

½ tsp thyme

Grind spices in food processor or coffee grinder. Store in an air-tight container.

SOUTHWEST SPICE

2 TBSP chili powder

1 TBSP dried oregano

2 TBSP paprika

1 TBSP ground coriander

1 TBSP garlic powder

1 TBSP salt

2 tsp ground cumin

1 tsp black pepper

1 tsp cayenne pepper

1 tsp ground red pepper

Combine all ingredients thoroughly and store in an airtight container.

GRAPEFRUIT VINAIGRETTE DRESSING

1/2 grapefruit
1 TBSP apple cider vinegar
Juice of ½ lemon
1/8 tsp salt
1/8 tsp pepper
Stevia to taste

Add all ingredients into a blender. Blend until the dressing reaches your desired consistency. Use immediately or store in an air-tight container for up to 3 days.
Serving Size – 1 Fruit, ½ Lemon

APPLE CIDER VINEGAR DRESSING

2/3 c. water
1/3 c. Apple Cider Vinegar
Stevia powder or liquid drops to taste
Salt and pepper to taste

Mix the water and apple cider vinegar together, stir or shake, and then add stevia drops or powder to taste into the mixture. Finally, pour over your lettuce. Store in fridge for up to 1 week.

ASIAN CITRUS DRESSING

¼ c. apple cider vinegar
1 c. water
1 TBSP fresh lemon juice
15 drops Clear stevia
10 drops Apricot Nectar flavored stevia
1 packet stevia
¼ tsp Chinese Style Five Spice (optional)
¼ tsp garlic salt (optional)
Dash of curry seasoning
Dash of cumin

Combine ingredients, pour into jar and refrigerate.

VINAIGRETTE DRESSING

¼ apple cider vinegar
1 c. water
Ground pepper to taste
20 drops Clear stevia
3 packets stevia

Combine ingredients, pour into jar and refrigerate.

STRAWBERRY VINAIGRETTE DRESSING

10 medium strawberries
1 TBSP apple cider vinegar
Juice of ½ lemon
1/8 tsp salt
1/8 tsp pepper
Stevia to taste

Add all ingredients into a blender. Blend until the dressing reaches your desired consistency. Use immediately or store in an air-tight container for up to 3 days.
Serving Size - 1 Fruit, ½ Lemon

Maintenance Recipes

Beverages (Maintenance) (10)

Carbonated water is not allowed while on the low calorie diet.

ROOT BEER
8 oz. carbonated water
15 drops Root Beer stevia

Mix in a glass over ice and enjoy.

CITRUS BURST
8 oz. carbonated water
10 drops Lemon Drop stevia
5 drops Apricot Nectar stevia

Mix in a glass over ice and enjoy.

GRAPE SODA
8 oz. carbonated water
10 drops Grape stevia

Mix in a glass over ice and enjoy.

MOCK 7-UP
8 oz. carbonated water
10 drops Lemon Drop stevia
Juice from a lime, to taste

Mix in a glass over ice and enjoy.

ROOT BEER CREME

8 oz. carbonated water

13 drops Root Beer stevia

3 drops Vanilla Crème stevia

Mix in a glass over ice and enjoy.

ORANGE SODA

8 oz. carbonated water

15 drops Valencia Orange stevia

Mix in a glass over ice and enjoy.

MOCK FRESCA

8 oz. carbonated water

10 drops Lemon Drop stevia

Mix in a glass over ice and enjoy.

STRAWBERRY ORANGE SMOOTHIE

¾ c. crushed ice

1 orange

1 c. fresh or partially defrosted strawberries

5 drops stevia

5 drops Valencia Orange stevia

5 drops Vanilla Crème stevia

Mix in a blender and serve in a tall glass. You can garnish with a lemon, lime, or an orange wedge.

GOOD FOR YOU LEMONADE
4 medium carrots
½ medium lemon, peeled
1 apple
½ c. red cabbage
1 tsp ginger

Place all ingredients in a juicer or blender. Serve over ice.

KICKSTART MY DAY SMOOTHIE
1 medium bananas, peeled
1 medium cucumber
2 TBSP fresh basil
1 TBSP fresh mint
1 apple
1 peach, pitted
Ice, as needed

Place all ingredients in a blender and serve.

Fish and Seafood (Maintenance) (10)

SHRIMP CEVICHE

1 to 2 lbs. shrimp, peeled and deveined, tail-on or off
2 large lemons, freshly squeezed
2-3 large limes, freshly squeezed
1 TBSP fresh garlic, minced
1 mild to medium pepper, ribs and seeds removed, finely chopped
1 red onion, finely chopped
1-3 TBSP Tabasco or hot sauce
4 large tomatoes
2 cucumbers, peeled and diced into 1/2 inch pieces fresh
½ c. each of freshly chopped cilantro and parsley
Sea salt and fresh ground black pepper to taste

Thaw shrimp if frozen. If using raw shrimp, bring a pot of water to boil and cook the shrimp for a minute or two until it turns opaque and reddish—do not over cook the shrimp as it will be too rubbery in texture. Rinse shrimp under cold water. Combine juices of lemons and limes in a large bowl (not metal) or large sandwich baggie and add shrimp. Cover bowl or seal baggie and refrigerate for 30 minutes to marinade. Large shrimp could be cut into smaller chunks (remove tails if doing this) to speed up marinade time. Add to shrimp the Tabasco, garlic, onion and pepper and toss/mix evenly. Return to refrigerator for another 30 minutes to let the flavors infuse the shrimp. Before serving, toss in a bowl the marinated shrimp mixture, cilantro, parsley, tomatoes and cucumbers and if needed, add sea salt and black pepper to taste.

SALMON WITH FRESH HERBS

1 lb. skinless salmon fillet, split into 4 portions
1 lemon
1 TBSP fresh dill
1 TBSP fresh lemon thyme
1 TBSP parsley
½ tsp salt
½ tsp pepper
2 TBSP butter, softened
Zucchini, sliced

Preheat oven to 350. Rinse salmon and pat dry. Cut lemon in half, and then shred 1 tsp. of lemon peel. In a bowl, add lemon peel, herbs, salt, pepper and softened butter, mix well. Spread onto salmon. In an oven-safe pan warmed over medium heat, add salmon with the herb side down. Cook until golden brown. Turn salmon over and squeeze the juice of ½ lemon onto fish. Place the pan in the oven for about 7 minutes, or until the fish flakes. While the fish is cooking, steam the zucchini. When the salmon is done, place it on a plate and top with lemon peel and herbs if you'd like. Serve with steamed zucchini.

TUNA KABOBS

2 lbs. tuna steak, cut into 1-inch cubes
1 onion, cut into 1-inch cubes
1 tomato, cut into 1-inch cubes
1 zucchini, cut into 1-inch cubes
1 yellow squash, cut into 1-inch cubes
1 green bell pepper, cut into 1-inch cubes
Juice of 1 lime
1 tsp cumin
1 tsp coriander

In a bowl, add lime juice, cumin & coriander. Place cubed tuna in bowl and mix gently until the tuna is covered with sauce. Set aside. If using wooden skewers, make sure to soak them for 20 minutes before placing food on them. Once skewers and tuna are ready, start placing food on the skewers, alternating between vegetables and tuna. Once ready, grill tuna until thoroughly cooked. Serve.

SPINACH STUFFED FISH FILETS

1 lb. fish of your choice
1 c. baby spinach, chopped into smaller pieces
½ c. feta cheese crumbles
Salt & pepper to taste
½ tsp garlic powder
½ tsp onion powder

Carefully cut small pocket in each filet of fish. In a small bowl, mix spinach and feta cheese together. Carefully stuff spinach mixture into each filet. Sprinkle with salt, pepper, garlic powder and onion powder. On a BBQ, grill for 10 minutes, 5 minutes each side or until fish flakes.

HOT & SPICY SWORDFISH

Juice of 1 lime
1 tsp salt
1/8 tsp black pepper
¼ tsp ginger
¼ tsp basil
¼ tsp paprika
1/8 tsp cayenne pepper
1/8 tsp thyme
1/8 tsp parsley
1 tsp Sriracha hot sauce
3 TBSP vegetable oil
1 lb. swordfish filets

In a medium bowl, add all ingredients except swordfish. Mix well, and then add the fish. Cover fish with marinade, and then place in the refrigerator for 1 hour. Place fish in the broiler, cooking for about 10 minutes, flipping once during cooking. Fish is done when it flakes easily. Serve.

SHRIMP SCAMPI

¼ c. butter
6 tsp garlic, minced
1 lb. shrimp

In a frying pan, melt butter over medium-high heat. Once butter is melted, add garlic and cook for 3 minutes. Add shrimp and cook until done. Serve.

TEX-MEX SALMON

2 avocados, pitted and diced
1 medium tomato, diced
2 cloves garlic, minced
3 TBSP sugar-free Greek yogurt
1 TBSP lemon juice
2 lbs. salmon steak
2 tsp dill weed
3 tsp lemon pepper, divided
Salt & pepper to taste
2 c. shredded cabbage
¼ c. water

Preheat BBQ while preparing meal. To make the avocado yogurt sauce, mash avocados, garlic, yogurt, and lemon juice together. Add salt and pepper to taste. Gently mix in tomatoes. Set aside. Season the salmon with dill weed, 2 tsp. lemon pepper, salt and pepper. Cook salmon on BBQ until flakey, turning once. While cooking the salmon, place shredded cabbage in a frying pan with water and 1 tsp. lemon pepper. 'Fry' cabbage until done to desired tenderness. Place cabbage on a plate, top with salmon and serve with a side of avocado yogurt sauce.

SWEET & TANGY TUNA STEAKS

Juice of 1 orange
¼ c. soy sauce (no added sugar)
2 TBSP olive oil
Juice of ½ lemon
2 tsp parsley
1 clove garlic, minced
¼ tsp oregano
½ tsp lemon pepper
½ tsp basil
1 lb. tuna steaks
1 lemon, cut into wedges

In a medium bowl, mix all ingredients except lemon wedges and tuna steaks. Reserve ½ cup of marinade for brushing the tuna while grilling. Pour remaining marinade in a gallon size sandwich bag; add the tuna steaks and seal. Lightly move bag so tuna is covered in marinade. Marinate for 1 hour in the refrigerator. Heat BBQ grill and place tuna steaks on the grill. While cooking, brush tuna with reserved marinade. Cook until they reach your desired doneness. Serve with lemon wedges on the side.

ITALIAN BAKED HALIBUT

1 tsp olive oil

1 c. zucchini, diced

½ c. onion, minced

1 clove garlic, minced

1 15oz can diced tomatoes, no sugar added

2 TBSP fresh basil, chopped

¼ tsp salt

¼ tsp black pepper

¼ tsp oregano

¼ tsp parsley

1 ½ lbs. halibut steaks

1/3 c. feta cheese crumbles, no sugar added

Preheat oven to 450. In a saucepan, heat oil over medium heat. Once warm, add zucchini, onion and garlic. Cook until tender. Once done, place in a small bowl. Add tomatoes, and all spices. Mix well. In the bottom of a shallow baking dish, place halibut steaks on the bottom, then cover with vegetable mixture, followed by topping with feta cheese. Bake for about 15 minutes until the halibut easily flakes, then serve.

ALMOND CRUSTED SALMON

1 lb. salmon filets

2 tsp sun-dried tomatoes

Salt & Pepper to taste

½ c. crushed raw almonds

In a small bowl, mix tomatoes, salt, pepper and almonds. Cover salmon with almond mixture. Place in a broiler pan sprayed with non-stick spray. Cook for 8-10 minutes, until the salmon easily flakes. Serve.

Chicken (Maintenance) (10)

SALSA CHICKEN

100 grams chicken breast
Salsa with no added sugars or preservatives

Place chicken in crockpot with salsa. Cook for 6 hours on low.

MEXICAN CHICKEN LETTUCE WRAPS

100 grams chicken breast – chopped
¼ c. organic chicken broth
¼ c. finely diced white onion
1 garlic clove, pressed
Fresh herbs to taste (cilantro, oregano, parsley)
Dried spices to taste (cumin, chili powder, salt, pepper)
2 large butter leaf lettuce leaves (for taco shells)

In a small pan, sauté onions, garlic and spices (not herbs) in the chicken broth. When onions are starting to caramelize, add chicken. Cook completely. Spoon out mixture into large butter leaves and garnish with fresh herbs. Add fresh organic, sugar free salsa if desired.

DEEP DISH QUICHE

4 oz. sugar free cream cheese
4 large eggs
¼ c. Parmesan cheese
1/3 c. heavy cream
½ tsp oregano
2 c. Italian cheese, shredded
½ tsp garlic, minced
¼ c. sugar free tomato sauce
1 c. mozzarella cheese
Your favorite toppings such as grilled chicken, onions and mushrooms

In a medium bowl, beat cream and eggs until smooth. Add cream cheese, Parmesan, oregano and garlic. Grease a 9" baking dish. Put 2 cups Italian cheese in a dish and pour egg mixture over the cheese. Lightly mix. Bake at 375 for 30 minutes. After 30 minutes, remove quiche from oven and spread with tomato sauce, mozzarella cheese and toppings. Bake for another 10 minutes until the cheese is bubbling.

BREAKFAST SAUSAGE PATTIES

1 lb. ground chicken breast (can use ground turkey as well)
2 TBSP Italian Seasoning
2 TBSP onion powder
2 TBSP garlic powder
½ tsp cayenne powder
¼ tsp salt
¼ tsp pepper

Place chicken breast in a large bowl and add all spices. Mix all ingredients together. Form into 2-inch patties. Cook in a frying pan over medium heat. Add a little olive oil if the patties are sticking to the pan. Cook until golden brown on each side.

CURRY CHICKEN

1 lb. chicken breast, cut into 1-inch pieces
1 medium onion, chopped
1 c. cauliflower
Olive oil
2 TBSP curry powder
2 tsp ginger
½ tsp salt
¼ c. water

Sauté the onion and spices in olive oil, until the onion is soft. Add chicken. When the chicken is done, add cauliflower. Stir well and add ¼ c. of water. Cover and cook on low heat for about 7 minutes, stirring occasionally. Serve once the cauliflower is to your desired tenderness.

STUFFED CHICKEN BREASTS
1 lb. chicken breast
1 8oz can mushrooms
½ c. feta cheese crumbles
Salt & pepper to taste
½ tsp garlic powder
½ tsp onion powder

Carefully cut a small pocket in each chicken breast. In a small bowl, mix mushrooms and feta cheese together. Carefully stuff mushroom mixture into each chicken breast. Sprinkle with salt, pepper, garlic powder and onion powder. On the BBQ, cook for about 15 minutes, occasionally turning chicken breast, until done.

TANGY CHICKEN BREAST
2 TBSP coconut or canola oil
2 lbs. chicken breast
4 c. tomato sauce (sugar-free)
2 cloves garlic, minced
¼ c. dried onion flakes
2 bay leaves
½ tsp cumin
1 tsp oregano
1 TBSP apple cider vinegar
Fresh parsley

In a frying pan, warm oil over medium heat. Cook chicken until brown on both sides. In a medium bowl, mix together tomato sauce, garlic, onion, bay leaves, cumin, oregano and vinegar. Add sauce to frying pan and bring to a light boil. Reduce heat if needed; allow chicken to simmer until no longer pink in the middle.

SPICY WHOLE CHICKEN

1 whole chicken (about 3lbs)
1 TBSP olive oil
½ tsp salt
½ tsp black pepper
1 tsp oregano
1 tsp basil
1 tsp paprika
2 tsp cayenne pepper
2 lemons
1 TBSP sugar-free hot sauce

Preheat oven to 450. Rinse chicken and remove all fat. Place chicken in small baking pan and rub with oil. In a small bowl, mix all seasonings including juice of 2 lemons. Rub on chicken, including the inside. Once lemons are juiced, cut into quarters and place around the chicken and inside for extra flavor. Roast for 20 minutes, then lower heat to 400 and roast another 40 minutes, or until chicken is done. Cool for 10 minutes before serving.

CHICKEN & MUSHROOMS

4 boneless chicken breasts
1 c. mushrooms
½ c. butter
1 tsp thyme
1 tsp parsley
1 tsp rosemary
1 tsp basil
½ pint whipping cream
Salt & pepper to taste

In a frying pan, melt butter. Cook chicken in butter until no longer pink. Remove chicken from pan. Sprinkle chicken breasts with thyme, parsley, rosemary and basil. Add mushrooms to pan with butter and sauté until done. When mushrooms are cooked, add chicken back to pan along with whipping cream. Cook until the cream is thicker, then season with salt & pepper. Serve.

BASIL CHICKEN

4 chicken breasts
2 TBSP fresh basil
1 TBSP parsley
1 TBSP olive oil
1 TBSP dry mustard
Juice of 1 lemon
¼ tsp salt/pepper

In a gallon sandwich bag, add all ingredients except chicken. Mix well, and then add chicken. Ensure the chicken is covered in marinade. Marinate the chicken in the fridge for 1–2 hours. Remove from bag and BBQ until no longer pink.

Beef (Maintenance) (10)

GROUND BEEF TACOS
1 lb. Extra Lean Ground Beef
½ tsp cumin
¼ tsp salt
¼ tsp black pepper
¼ tsp chili pepper
¼ tsp onion powder
¼ tsp garlic powder
1 Roma tomato, diced
1 avocado, sliced
½ red onion, diced
Romaine Lettuce, complete leaves

Cook beef thoroughly, and drain. Mix the cumin, black pepper, chili pepper, onion salt, and garlic powder in a bowl. Add seasonings to the ground beef. Add enough to season the meat to your taste. Then add a dash of regular salt if needed. Cut up Roma tomato, slice up avocado and dice up the red onion and set aside. Take leaves of romaine lettuce. Add some meat and the tomatoes, onion and avocado (and cheese if preferred) and eat it like a taco.

FAJITAS

1 ½ lbs. chicken or beef
1 medium onion, sliced
1 green bell pepper, sliced
2 c. mushrooms, sliced
1 clove garlic, minced
1 c. sugar free beef broth
¼ tsp paprika, pepper, salt and cayenne
Salsa & sour cream (optional)

In a cast iron skillet, grill chicken or beef, add garlic, onions, and bell pepper. Add paprika, cracked pepper, salt and cayenne. Add broth and cover. Cook for 20 minutes over medium heat. Serve with no added sugar salsa and sour cream.

CROCKPOT STEAK AND VEGETABLES

1 lb stew beef
1 TBSP HCG Friendly Shake N Bake (Found under 'Sauces, Rubs, Dressings and Marinades section)
4 cloves garlic, minced
1 c. celery, sliced
1 tomato, diced
1 onion, sliced
1 c. sugar free beef broth

Place all ingredients in a crockpot, starting with the beef on the bottom. Cover and cook on low for 8 hours. Serve.

MARINATED STEAK

2 lbs. steak
20 drops stevia
2 TBSP lemon juice
2 TSP olive oil
2 cloves garlic, minced
1 tsp ginger
½ tsp black pepper
½ tsp red pepper
½ tsp onion flakes

In a sandwich bag, add all ingredients except for the steak. Seal and mix ingredients. Add steak and seal bag. Mix so steak is covered in sauce. Refrigerate in sandwich bag overnight. Cook on BBQ when ready.

CORNED BEEF & CABBAGE

4 lb. corned beef
1 onion
1 bag of baby carrots
1 head of cabbage
3 cloves garlic – sliced
3 bay leaves
10 peppercorns
1 lb. cauliflower

In a slow cooker, place carrots and cauliflower on the bottom. Top with corned beef. Add sliced onion, garlic, bay leaves and peppercorns to crock-pot. Cover corned beef with water. Cook on low for 8 hours, high for 6 hours. About half way through cooking, cut cabbage into eighths and add to crockpot. Serve when done.

SHEPHARD'S PIE

1 lb. ground beef
1 lb. cauliflower
½ c. sliced carrots
½ c. sliced celery
½ onion, chopped
2 cloves garlic, minced
1 tsp pepper
1 tsp salt
1 c. milk
2 c. cheddar cheese, shredded

Preheat oven to 350. In a frying pan, cook beef until done with onion. Once the beef is done, start steaming cauliflower in a steamer. While the cauliflower is steaming, add carrots, celery and spices into the beef mixture. Cook this mixture for about 5 minutes, or until the carrots are starting to get tender. Once the beef mixture is done, place this mix into a greased 2-quart casserole dish. Once the cauliflower is steamed, place in a bowl and add milk. With a hand mixer or potato smasher, mash cauliflower until it reaches the consistency of mashed potatoes. Pour cauliflower onto beef mixture and spread evenly. Top with cheese. Bake at 350 for 30 minutes.

BEEF STROGANOFF

1 lb stew beef
1 lb cauliflower
6 TBSP butter
1 c. mushrooms, sliced
2 cloves garlic, minced
½ medium onion, minced
¼ tsp pepper
¼ tsp salt
½ can sugar free beef broth
1 c. sour cream

In a frying pan, add 2 TBSP butter, beef, garlic, pepper and salt. Cook until beef is done. While beef is cooking, steam cauliflower. Add onions, mushrooms and remaining 4 TBSP of butter to frying pan. Cook until butter is melted and onions are transparent. Add beef broth; stir until it slowly starts to thicken. Then add sour cream and stir thoroughly. Serve over steamed cauliflower.

SOUTHWESTERN STEAK

2 lbs. rib eye steak
8 cloves garlic, minced
6 TBSP kosher salt
6 TBSP canola oil
2 TBSP chili powder
2 TBSP cumin

In a bowl, add all the spices and oil together, mix well. Rub paste over both sides of steak. Cook on a BBQ until done to desired doneness and serve.

BEEF & BROCCOLI FRITTATA

½ lb. of broccoli
½ lb. of spinach
1 lb. stew beef
½ onion, diced
1 TBSP butter
8 Eggs
1 c. Milk
3 oz. parmesan cheese
2 c. Mozzarella
Salt, pepper and basil to taste

Preheat oven to 350 degrees. Sauté the broccoli, spinach, beef and onion together in 1 TBSP of butter until they are tender. While that is cooking, beat eggs in a bowl, and then add a cup of milk to it and about 3 oz. of Parmesan cheese along with some salt/pepper and basil. After the veggies are steamed and sautéed, then spray a 13 x 9 baking dish with non-stick cooking spray and put the veggies on the bottom making it as even as possible. Pour the egg, cheese, spices, and milk mixture over veggies. Then sprinkle 2 handfuls of mozzarella cheese over the top. Bake, uncovered for about 20 minutes. The eggs should NOT be all the way set. Then switch the oven over to BROIL and watch closely until the cheese starts to bubble. Remove and cool, cut frittata into serving squares. Put them in individual sandwich bags and freeze, if you have leftovers.

STUFFED BURGERS

2 lbs. ground beef
1 tsp cumin
1 tsp garlic powder
1 tsp onion powder
½ tsp white pepper
½ tsp salt
½ lb. Gouda cheese, sliced
Romaine lettuce leaves

In a mixing bowl, add ground beef and spices. Mix well. Form into ¼ lb. burger patties. Place 2oz of Gouda cheese on top of one patty, then place a 2nd patty on top, forming a seal around the edge. Cook burgers until they are at your desired doneness. Place in a romaine lettuce leaf and serve.

Vegetables (Maintenance) (10)

FRITTATA

1 lb. of vegetables (broccoli, spinach, etc.)
½ onion, diced
1 c. mushrooms, sliced
8 Eggs
1 c. Milk
¼ c. Parmesan cheese
2 c. Mozzarella
Salt, pepper and basil to taste
1 TBSP butter

Preheat the oven to 350 degrees. Sauté onions and mushrooms in 1 TBSP of butter until they are tender. Steam other veggies such as broccoli and spinach until they reach your desired consistency. While those are cooking, beat eggs in a bowl, and then add a cup of milk and the Parmesan cheese along with some salt/pepper and some basil. After the veggies are steamed and sautéed, spray a 13 x 9 baking dish with non-stick cooking spray and put the veggies on the bottom making it as even as possible. Pour the egg, cheese, spices, and milk mixture over veggies. Then sprinkle 2 handfuls of mozzarella cheese over the top. Bake, uncovered for about 20 minutes. The eggs should NOT be all the way set. Then switch the oven over to BROIL and watch closely until the cheese starts to bubble. Remove and cool, cut frittata into serving squares. Put them in individual sandwich bags and freeze, if you have leftovers.

STEAMED KALE

1 bunch of fresh kale, chopped
¼ onion, chopped
2 garlic cloves, minced
1 c. water
Braggs liquid aminos
Salt and Pepper to taste

Place the onion, garlic, kale, salt, pepper and water in large pan. Bring to a boil. Cover and simmer for about 30 minutes (until kale is tender). Sprinkle with liquid aminos.

FAUX MASHED POTATOES

1 lb. cauliflower
1 TBSP water
1 TBSP butter
1–2 TBSP heavy cream
Salt and pepper to taste

Chop the cauliflower into small pieces and place in large covered casserole dish. Add water and microwave on high for 5 minutes. Stir and microwave for an additional 5 minutes. Remove and let stand covered for 5 more minutes, then drain. Place in a food processor or blender with butter and heavy cream. Process until smooth and creamy, scraping down the sides of the processor occasionally. Season the cauliflower with salt and pepper.

ROASTED VEGETABLES

1 medium purple onion
1 lb. asparagus
1 lb. mushrooms, any variety
1 yellow bell pepper
1 orange bell pepper
2 medium tomatoes, seeded
1 zucchini
1 yellow squash
Olive oil
Salt and pepper to taste

Preheat oven to 350 degrees. Wash and chop the veggies into big, but bite-size pieces. Add all veggies to a bowl. Drizzle with olive oil and salt/pepper. Use a spatula to thoroughly coat veggies. Spread veggies into a shallow baking dish. Bake uncovered until veggies are tender, about 30 minutes.

FRIED ZUCCHINI

2 c. zucchini, grated
2 eggs, beaten
¼ c. onion, chopped
½ c. Parmesan cheese, grated
½ c. mozzarella cheese, grated
½ tsp parsley
½ tsp cayenne pepper
Salt and pepper to taste
2 TBSP canola oil

In a medium bowl, shred zucchini with a cheese grater for a total of 2 cups. Add eggs, onion, cheeses, and spices. Mix well. Add oil to a frying pan and heat until warm. Drop zucchini into frying pan, using a spoon. There should be about 1-2 tablespoons per patty. Cook for 2-3 minutes on each side, until golden brown. Serve.

SWEET & ZESTY CARROTS

2 lbs. baby carrots
3 TBSP butter
¼ tsp ground nutmeg
¼ tsp salt
1 tsp orange zest
2 tsp lemon juice
Fresh parsley, chopped

Add carrots into a pot of water. Boil until carrots are tender. In a frying pan, melt butter, and then add nutmeg, salt, orange zest and lemon juice. Once mixed together, add carrots and lightly coat. Place carrots on a serving dish and top with parsley.

EGGPLANT KEBOBS

1 medium eggplant, cut into 1-inch cubes
1 large red onion, cut into 8 pieces
2 large tomatoes, quartered
3 TBSP lemon juice
1 TBSP lime juice
1 tsp cumin
½ tsp paprika
¼ tsp cayenne
3 ½ TBSP olive oil
2 tsp garlic, minced
½ cup plain Greek yogurt
Canola oil
Salt and pepper to taste

Brush grill with canola oil so the eggplant doesn't stick.
Mix yogurt, 1 tsp garlic and lime juice in a small bowl. Add
salt and pepper to taste. In a separate bowl, whisk
together olive oil, lemon juice, cumin, paprika, cayenne
and garlic. Add eggplant, onion and tomato, toss to coat.
Place vegetables on a skewer; it'll make approximately 4
skewers total. Grill for 6 minutes on each side, until
eggplant is tender. Serve with yogurt sauce.

SPAGHETTI SQUASH WITH FETA CHEESE

1 spaghetti squash, halved lengthwise and seeds removed
2 TBSP canola oil
1 onion, chopped
1 clove garlic, minced
1 ½ c. diced tomatoes
¾ c. feta cheese (check for sugars)
3 TBSP sliced olives
2 TBSP fresh basil, chopped
Salt and pepper to taste

Preheat oven to 350. Place squash, cut sides down on a baking sheet, and cook for 30 minutes. Remove from oven and set aside. While the squash is cooking, heat oil in a frying pan. Sauté onion and garlic in the frying pan for about 3–5 minutes. Add tomatoes and cook until tomatoes are warm. Using a spoon, scoop out insides of spaghetti squash into a bowl. Add vegetables, feta cheese, olives, and spices. Mix well and serve.

SPINACH ARTICHOKE DIP

8 oz. cream cheese, softened
2 c. mozzarella, shredded
½ c. Parmesan
10 oz. frozen spinach
4 TBSP sugar free mayo
1 c. sugar free sour cream
1 tsp salt
1 tsp olive oil
1 tsp red pepper flakes

Preheat oven to 350. In a large frying pan, heat olive oil. Drain spinach and pat dry. Add spinach and salt to pan. In the meantime, mix mozzarella, sour cream, mayo and cream cheese in a bowl. Add cream mixture to pan with spinach and salt. Stir well. Spray a glass-baking dish with non-stick spray and pour mixture into dish. Sprinkle the top with Parmesan and bake for 30 minutes. Serve immediately with celery and carrots.

ZUCCHINI CASSEROLE

4 medium zucchini, sliced thinly
2 TBSP butter
½ onion, diced
2 cloves garlic, minced
½ c. heavy cream
½ c. Parmesan cheese, shredded
Salt and pepper to taste
1 tsp parsley
1 tsp basil

Preheat oven to 450. In a large pan, melt butter, and then add zucchini, onion, and garlic. Season the zucchini with salt, pepper, parsley and basil. Continue to stir until zucchini is tender, for about 5 minutes. Add the heavy cream and cook until thick. Remove pan from heat and stir in cheese. Spoon zucchini mixture into a 2 quart baking dish, and then sprinkle with Parmesan cheese and cook for about 8-10 minutes.

Soups (Maintenance) (10)

VEGETARIAN CHOWDER

1 medium onion, chopped
3-4 celery stalks, chopped
½ c. bell pepper, chopped
2 c. cauliflower, chopped
3 c. of broccoli, chopped
¼ head of green cabbage, chopped
10 Crimini mushrooms, chopped
2- 3 cloves of garlic
2 TBSP butter
1 qt. half and half milk
1 qt. chicken stock
2 ½ c. medium cheddar, shredded

Sauté onion, celery and green pepper in a frying pan. Once softened, add 2-3 cloves of garlic. Cook until garlic is incorporated. Move to your main pot. In a steamer, steam cauliflower, broccoli, green cabbage and mushrooms together for 10 minutes. Puree half of the steamed veggies. Mix them with the other veggie mix in the main pot. In a frying pan add 2 TBSP of butter. Heat through then add ¾ qt. of half & half, salt and pepper to make a rue. Stir until smooth then add 1 ½ c. of shredded cheese and 1 ½ c. chicken stock. Add garlic powder and onion powder. Then add 1 tsp pepper, ½ tsp seasoning salt and sea salt. Stir until smooth and pour over veggies in the main pot. Simmer over medium until desired consistency. Add remaining milk or additional chicken stock to thin.

HOMEMADE TOMATO SOUP

2 c. diced tomatoes
¾ c. olive oil
½ c. celery, diced
½ c. carrots, diced
1 yellow onion, diced
2 cloves garlic, minced
1 c. chicken broth
½ tsp Italian seasoning
Salt & pepper to taste
1 bay leaf
2 TBSP butter
¼ c. fresh basil leaves, chopped
½ c. heavy cream

Preheat oven to 450. Dice tomatoes and strain the juices, setting the juice aside. Spread the tomatoes on a baking sheet, season with salt & pepper and drizzle with ¼ c. of olive oil. Roast for about 15 minutes. While the tomatoes are roasting, heat remaining olive oil over medium heat in a saucepan. Add celery, carrot, onion, and garlic. Cook until tender, about 10 minutes. Once veggies are done, add tomatoes, tomato juice, chicken broth, spices (except basil) and butter to the pan. Simmer for about 15–20 minutes. Add basil and cream, and heat until warm. Once done, place soup in a blender until it reaches your desired consistency. Serve.

SPAGHETTI SQUASH SOUP

3 small spaghetti squash, cut in halves lengthwise, seeds removed
2 TBSP butter
1 TBSP olive oil
1 small onion, diced
1 c. carrots, thinly sliced
8 c. chicken broth
½ tsp fresh sage
½ tsp thyme
Salt and pepper to taste

Preheat oven to 375. Place squash cut sides down on a baking sheet. Cook for 50 minutes and then allow to cool. In a large pot, melt butter and add olive oil. Cook the onion and carrot until tender. Add chicken broth, sage and thyme. Simmer for 20 minutes, adding salt and pepper to taste. Remove the inside of 2 halves of the spaghetti squash into the broth. Cook until warm, stirring occasionally. Place the 4 spaghetti squash halves into their own bowls. Slowly pour soup into each half of the squash. Sprinkle with salt, pepper and Parmesan cheese.

VEGETABLE CHILI

1 red bell pepper, seeded & diced
1 small eggplant, cubed
1 medium onion, diced
2 medium zucchini, cubed
1 tomato, diced
1 TBSP olive oil
½ tsp salt
2 cloves garlic, minced
1 lb. mushrooms, quartered
1 bay leaf
1 tsp. chili powder
2 c. vegetable broth (no sugar added)

In a frying pan, heat oil over medium heat. Add vegetables and sauté until tender. Once the veggies are done, add them into a large pot, and add salt, garlic, bay leaf, chili powder, and broth. Simmer for 45 minutes and serve.

ASIAN ONION SOUP

2 c. green onions, chopped
1 TBSP butter
1 TBSP olive oil
1 onion, chopped
3 TBSP orange juice
6 c. beef broth (sugar free)
1 TBSP lemon juice
¼ tsp salt and pepper
1 clove garlic, minced

Fill a large bowl with water and ice, and then set aside. In a large pot of boiling water, add green onions and cook for 1 minute. Move green onions to the ice bath. Once they are cooled, drain and set aside. In a saucepan, add 1 TBSP butter and olive oil. Add onion and cook for about 8 minutes. Add orange juice and beef broth. Simmer for 20 minutes. Stir in lemon juice, garlic, salt & pepper. Add green onions to the soup and serve.

CAULIFLOWER CHEESE SOUP

3 c. cauliflower flowerettes (can also use broccoli)
1 medium onion, chopped
1 carrot, chopped
4 cups chicken broth
½ tsp cayenne
1 clove garlic, minced
½ tsp Worcestershire sauce (no sugar added)
1 c. cheddar cheese, grated
Salt & pepper, to taste
2 c. light cream

Combine cauliflower, onion, carrot, chicken broth and spices to crock-pot. Cover and cook on low for 6 hours. Once done, puree in a blender until it reaches your desired consistency. Return to crock-pot and mix in light cream, Worcestershire, and cheese. Cook for 1 more hour on low, and then serve.

ALBONDIGAS SOUP

1 serving meatballs
2-3 c. beef or chicken broth
1 c. bok choy
½ c. onions
Fresh cilantro, chopped
Seasonings to taste

In a saucepan, bring broth to a boil. Feel free to add any seasonings you like to taste (oregano, basil, pepper, garlic, etc.). I'll usually add in some hot sauce or Tabasco. Add cooked meatballs and veggies. Cover & simmer 20-30 minutes or until vegetables reach desired tenderness. Top with fresh chopped cilantro. Serve.

SPLIT PEA SOUP

1 lb dried green split peas, rinsed

2 ham hocks

3 carrots, peeled & sliced

½ c. onion, chopped

2 ribs celery, chopped

2 cloves garlic, minced

1 bay leaf

2 tsp dried parsley flakes

1 tsp oregano

½ tsp cayenne

1 TBSP Old Bay Seasoning

½ tsp fresh pepper

1 ½ qts water

Place all ingredients in a slow cooker. Cover and cook on high for 4 hours or low for 8 hours, until peas are soft. Remove ham hock and bay leaves. Mash peas until you reach desired consistency. Serve.

VEGETABLE GUMBO

1 c. vegetable broth
½ c. onion, chopped
¼ c. green bell pepper, chopped
2 ribs celery, chopped
1 clove garlic, minced
1 lb. okra
1 lb. tomatoes, chopped
2 c. corn kernels
¼ tsp Tabasco
¼ tsp paprika
¼ tsp Old Bay Seasoning
2 TBSP parsley, chopped
1 TBSP, basil chopped
Salt and pepper to taste

In a slow cooker, add broth, onion, green pepper, celery and garlic. Cook on low for 3 hours. Add okra, tomatoes, corn, Tabasco, paprika, Old Bay, parsley, basil, salt and pepper. Cook for another 2–3 hours on low. Serve.

LEFTOVER TURKEY SOUP

2 c. water or chicken broth
10–12 oz. turkey breast
1 large onion, chopped
3 celery sticks, shopped
2 c. tomatoes, chopped
2 TBSP garlic, minced
½ pkg frozen chopped spinach, thawed and drained
1 TBSP chopped parsley
1/8 tsp marjoram
1 bay leaf
1/8 tsp Your HCG Basic Seasoning (Found under 'Sauces, Rubs, Dressings and Marinades section)
1/8 tsp thyme
Salt and pepper to taste

Combine all ingredients except parsley (if using fresh) and spinach in crock-pot. Cook on low for 8 hours or 4 hours on high. When there is one hour left before serving, add spinach and fresh parsley. Salt and pepper to taste.

Salads (Maintenance) (10)

YOURHCG.COM CHEF SALAD
2 c. lettuce
1 tomato, chopped
½ cucumber, sliced and seeded
¼ c. ham
¼ c. turkey
2 hard-boiled eggs
Favorite YourHCG.com dressing

Place all of the ingredients on a plate and enjoy.

GRILLED CHICKEN SALAD

2 c. lettuce
2 TBSP blue cheese crumbles
4 oz. chicken breast, chopped
½ c. apple slices
2 TBSP sliced raw almonds
½ c. tomatoes, chopped
Favorite YourHCG.com dressing

Place all of the ingredients on a plate and serve.

GREEK SALAD

2 c. romaine lettuce
1 tomato, chopped into chunks
½ red onion, thinly sliced
½ cucumber, cut into 1-inch chunks
1 small red bell pepper, seeded and cut into chunks
1 small green bell pepper, seeded and cut into chunks
½ c. black olives
1 TBSP fresh parsley
4 oz. shrimp or chicken
¼ c. feta cheese
¼ c. olive oil
1 tsp dried oregano
Salt and pepper to taste

In a bowl, add lettuce, tomato, onion, cucumber, bell peppers, olives and parsley. Toss ingredients gently in bowl. In a small bowl, mix olive oil, oregano and salt & pepper to make a dressing. Place feta cheese and protein choice on top of lettuce, and then pour dressing over salad.

CHICKEN WALNUT SALAD

2 c. lettuce
4 oz. chicken breast, cooked
½ c. snow peas, chopped
½ c. red bell pepper, chopped
1 TBSP walnuts, chopped
Favorite YourHCG.com Dressing

Place all ingredients on a plate and serve.

WALDORF SALAD

½ c. walnuts, chopped
½ c. celery, sliced
½ c. grapes, sliced
1 apple, cored and chopped
3 TBSP mayo (Found under 'Sauces, Rubs, Dressings and Marinades section)
1 TBSP lemon juice
Salt and pepper to taste
¼ tsp celery salt
2 c. lettuce

In a bowl, combine mayo, salt, pepper, celery salt and lemon juice. Stir well. Add salt and pepper to taste. Add in apple, celery, grapes and walnuts. Mix well, covering all ingredients with mayo mixture. Serve on top of a bed of lettuce.

TUNA SALAD

4 oz. tuna, chopped (can also use chicken)
3 TBSP mayo (Found under 'Sauces, Rubs, Dressings and Marinades section)
1 tsp sugar free mustard
1 tsp sugar free relish
2 c. lettuce
½ c. tomato, chopped

In a small bowl, mix tuna, mayo, mustard and relish together. Place the lettuce and tomatoes on a plate. Top with tuna salad.

SALMON SALAD

4 oz. salmon, cooked

2 c. lettuce

½ c. green beans, sliced into ½ inch pieces

½ c. mushrooms

Favorite YourHCG.com Dressing

Place lettuce on a plate and top with salmon, green beans and mushrooms.

BUFFALO CHICKEN SALAD

4 oz. chicken, cooked

3 tsp Frank's Red Hot Sauce

2 c. lettuce of your choice

½ c. carrots, sliced

½ c. celery, sliced

¼ c. blue cheese crumbles

Favorite YourHCG.com Dressing (if needed)

In a pan, over medium heat, cook chicken until no longer pink. Once chicken is done, add Frank's red hot and cover chicken with sauce. On a plate, add lettuce, carrots, celery and blue cheese, then top with chicken. I used the juices from pan as dressing which will add some spice to your salad.

GRILLED STEAK SALAD

2 c. romaine
4 oz. grilled steak, cut into slices
½ c. carrots, sliced
½ c. tomatoes, chopped
Your HCG Greek Dressing

Place all ingredients on a plate and serve.

COBB SALAD

2 c. romaine lettuce
2 hard boiled eggs, sliced
1 avocado, sliced
½ c. blue cheese crumbles
4 oz. chicken breast, cooked

In a bowl, add all ingredients. Toss in the bowl gently and serve. Add one of the Your HCG dressings if needed.

'Breads' (Maintenance) (10)

OOPSIE ROLLS
3 large eggs
1/8 tsp salt
1/8 tsp cream of tartar
3 ounces cream cheese (Do not soften)

Preheat oven to 300. Separate the eggs. Add salt and cream cheese to the yolks. Use a mixer to combine the ingredients together. In a separate bowl, whip egg whites and cream of tartar until stiff (if you're using the same mixer, mix the whites first and then the yolk mixture). Using a spatula, gradually fold the egg yolk mixture into the white mixture, being careful not to break down the whites. Spray a cookie sheet with non-stick spray and spoon the mixture onto the sheet, making 6 mounds. Flatten each mound slightly. Bake on parchment paper about 30 minutes (You want them slightly softer, not crumbly). Let them cool on the sheet for a few minutes, and then remove to a rack and allow them to finish cooling. Store them in a bread sack or a sandwich bag.

PIZZA CRUST

2 c. mozzarella cheese
2 large eggs
2 TBSP flax seed meal
2 TBSP coconut flour
1/2 teaspoon baking soda

Mix all together. If you have a pizza stone, its good to use but if you don't just use a cookie sheet. Put the dough between two sheets of parchment paper and roll really thin, about a 1/4" thickness. Just make sure there are no holes in the dough. Remove the top sheet and bake at 350 for 15 minutes. Place the top sheet back on, flip and bake about 5-10 minutes more and then add your toppings. Bake or broil until bubbly.

PO' CAKES

2 eggs
7 TBSP almond flour
Pinch of salt

Heat skillet with oil. Mix eggs, flour and salt in a bowl until well blended. Drop by large spoonfuls and smooth out a bit. Cook on each side about 1-2 minutes until brown and a bit crunchy. Top with cream cheese or sugar free preserves of your choice.

VARIATION OF PO' CAKES

2 eggs
1/3 c. almond meal
Splash of milk
Pinch of salt
1 packet stevia

Preheat skillet with coconut oil. Mix eggs, almond meal, milk, salt and stevia in a bowl until well blended. In a frying pan or on a skillet, drop mixture making about 3 inch circles. Cook until light brown on one side, then flip until cooked all the way through.

CAULIFLOWER PIZZA CRUST

1 c. cauliflower, cooked
1 egg
1 c. mozzarella cheese
½ tsp fennel
1 tsp oregano
2 tsp parsley
Pizza or Alfredo sauce
Toppings (make sure meats are cooked)
Mozzarella cheese

Preheat oven to 450 degrees. Spray a cookie sheet with non-stick spray. In a medium bowl, combine cauliflower, egg and mozzarella. Move cauliflower mixture to a cookie sheet. Press evenly onto the bottom of the pan. Sprinkle evenly with fennel, oregano and parsley. Bake at 450 degrees for 12–15 minutes (15–20 minutes if you double the recipe). Remove the pan from the oven. To the crust, add sauce, then toppings and cheese. Place under a broiler at high heat just until cheese is melted.

CINNAMON BREAD

¼ c. flax seed meal
½ TBSP baking powder
1 TBSP cinnamon
1 tsp stevia
1 egg
1 TBSP butter, softened
Raisins (optional)

Mix dry ingredients together in a small bowl. In a coffee mug, mix softened butter and egg until well blended and not lumpy. Pour dry ingredients into mug and mix well. Microwave for 2 minutes, then serve.

CREAM CHEESE MUFFINS

8 oz. sugar free cream cheese, softened
1 large egg
1 tsp sugar free vanilla extract
3 TBSP stevia
Cinnamon

Preheat oven to 350. Line muffin pan with cupcake papers. Mix all ingredients together in a medium size bowl. Fill muffin cups about 2/3 full. Bake for 20 minutes.

CHEESE FILLED CREPES

2 eggs
2 TBSP ricotta cheese
½ tsp sugar-free vanilla
5 drops stevia
5 medium strawberries, sliced

In a medium sized bowl, mix eggs, cheese, vanilla and stevia together until well blended. Use a non-stick pan, sprayed with non-stick cooking spray. Once heated, pour batter into pan and cook on medium heat, then flip. Cook for 1-2 minutes. Top with strawberries and serve.

EASY BREAD RECIPE

2 ½ c. almond flour
½ tsp sea salt
½ tsp baking soda
3 eggs
1 TBSP agave nectar (use with caution)
½ tsp apple cider vinegar

Preheat oven to 300. In a large bowl, mix flour, salt and baking soda. In a separate bowl, mix eggs, agave nectar, and vinegar. Stir the wet ingredients into the bowl with the dry ingredients. Mix until well blended. Scoop batter into a bread pan. Bake for 45-55 minutes until thoroughly cooked. Cool and serve.

HERBED BREAD

2 c. flax meal
1 TBSP baking powder
½ tsp baking soda
Stevia, to taste
½ c. water
1/3 c. oil
5 eggs, beaten
1 tsp garlic, minced
1 TBSP basil
1 tsp rosemary
1 tsp thyme

Preheat oven to 350 and line baking sheet with parchment paper. Lightly oil parchment paper, so bread won't stick. In a large bowl, mix together flax seed, baking powder, baking soda and stevia. Add the water and oil, and mix well. Add the remaining ingredients, mix well, and then let them rest for five minutes. Spread the mixture on the baking sheet. Bake for about 25 minutes or until golden brown. Once cooked, you can cut into bread slices for sandwiches or sprinkle with Parmesan cheese and cook a little longer for a nice garlic bread.

Desserts and Fruits (Maintenance) (10)

CHEESECAKE

16 oz. cream cheese
12 packets stevia
3 large eggs
3 TBSP fresh lemon juice
1 ½ tsp vanilla extract – sugar free
¼ tsp salt
3 c. sour cream

Preheat the oven to 350. In a large mixing bowl, beat the cream cheese and sweetener until very smooth, about 3 minutes. Add the eggs, one at a time, beating well after each addition. Add the lemon juice, vanilla and salt. Beat in the sour cream until just blended. Grease an 8-inch Springform pan with 2 1/2 inch sides and line the bottom with greased parchment or wax paper. Wrap the outside of the pan with a double layer of heavy-duty foil to prevent leakage. Pour the batter into the pan. Set the pan in a large roasting pan and surround with 1 inch of very hot water. Bake for 45 minutes. Turn off the oven without opening the door and let the cake cool for 1 hour.
Remove to a rack and cool to room temperature, about 1 hour. Cover with plastic wrap and refrigerate overnight. Un-mold the cake onto a plate and serve.

APPLES WITH CREAMY STRAWBERRY SAUCE

1/2 Jonathon apple

3-5 medium strawberries

2 TBSP milk

3 drops Vanilla Creme stevia

Slice apple and arrange on a plate. Mash the strawberries with a fork and add Vanilla Creme stevia and milk to make a sauce. Pour over the apple slices.

MUG CAKE

4 TBSP almond flour

4 TBSP stevia

2 TBSP cocoa powder (may also use sugar free peanut butter or cinnamon)

1 egg

3 TBSP milk

3 TBSP oil

Splash of vanilla extract (sugar free)

Mix dry ingredients in a coffee mug, add egg and blend. Add milk, oil, vanilla and blend. Microwave for three minutes. Let cool and place on plate.

GLUTEN FREE ALMOND CREPES

1 1/2 c. water
6 eggs
1 1/2 c. almond flour
2-3 TBSP coconut flour
1/2 tsp sea salt

Preheat non-stick 10" skillet and coat with oil, spray, or butter. In a large bowl, beat together water, eggs, almond flour, coconut flour and salt. Allow batter to rest for 30 minutes. Mix batter for a few seconds before making each crepe as it separates very quickly. Pour about 3 TBSP of batter into the pan, and lift the pan and tip it around to distribute evenly. Cook on medium heat until light brown on the bottom. Do not try to remove too soon because they will collapse and be mushy. Gently slip a spatula under the crepe and flip. When done, turn out onto a clean kitchen towel to cool; afterward they can be stacked and won't stick to each other. You can lay them on a strong paper plate so they don't bend while storing and then put them in a sandwich bag in the fridge.

CHOCOLATE NIBLETS

3 TBSP butter
3 TBSP unsweetened cocoa powder
1 tsp stevia

In a saucepan, add butter, cocoa powder and stevia. Over medium heat, stir until melted and well blended. Pour onto parchment paper and place in freezer. Break into pieces.

DOUGHNUT HOLES

1 large egg
1/4 c. butter, melted
Stevia to taste
1 tsp vanilla
1 scoop Your HCG Vanilla Whey Protein Shake
Coconut oil
Cinnamon

Heat about 1 inch of oil in a heavy pan. While the oil is warming up, in a small bowl, mix together egg and melted butter. Once mixed well, add protein powder and vanilla. Mix well until the batter is no longer lumpy. Add stevia to taste. Let rest for 1-2 minutes, then mix again to make sure all lumps are gone. Using a spoon, drop batter into hot oil, 4 doughnut holes per pan. Fry until they are golden-brown, then turn. Drain on a paper towel, and then sprinkle with cinnamon.

PEANUT BUTTER CUPS

1 stick unsalted butter
1 oz. unsweetened chocolate
1 tsp stevia powder
1 TBSP heavy cream
4 TBSP peanut butter or almond butter (sugar free)
¼ c. raw almond slices

Melt butter, chocolate, and stevia in a double boiler. Once melted, stir in heavy cream and peanut/almond butter. Line a cupcake tin with cupcake papers. Place almond slices in bottom of cupcake papers. Spoon the chocolate mix into the tins. Place in the freezer until frozen. They are great right out of the freezer, because they do melt quickly.

ICE CREAM

1 c. heavy whipping cream
10 drops clear stevia
1 tsp sugar-free vanilla
1 handful of rock salt
Ice
1 TBSP sugar-free peanut butter

Add cream, sugar, vanilla and peanut butter into a small sandwich bag, and seal. In a gallon sized sandwich bag, fill ¾ full with ice and the handful of rock salt. Place the smaller bag in the larger bag and SHAKE! Shake for about 15 minutes or so. You can do it all yourself or have your family help you out. Remove smaller bag from larger back and enjoy!

BERRY SORBET

2 c. plain Greek yogurt (no sugar added)
¼ c. milk
¼ c. fresh raspberries
¼ c. fresh strawberries
1 TBSP fresh orange juice
¾ tsp powdered stevia
1 banana (optional)

Place all ingredients in a blender and blend until smooth.
Pour into 8oz Tupperware containers and freeze. Serve
once frozen.

PEANUT BUTTER FUDGE

1/3 c. boiling water

1 ¾ tsp liquid stevia

6 TBSP unsalted butter

1 ½ tsp vanilla extract, divided (not imitation)

1 c. instant nonfat dry milk

6 oz. unsweetened baking chocolate, chopped

1 c. peanut butter (sugar free)

½ c. raw peanuts, chopped

In a medium sized pot, bring water to a boil. Add the stevia, and mix well. Cut butter into 1 TBSP portions so they melt faster. Add the butter and stir until it is almost all melted. Add ½ tsp of vanilla and stir. Then pour mix into a mixing bowl. Add the dry milk and mix until blended. Place chocolate and peanut butter into a double boiler. Cook until melted and it is smooth when you stir. Add peanut butter mixture to milk bowl and blend until well mixed. Then add 1 tsp of vanilla and stir well. Line an 8x8 pan with foil, then pour fudge into it. Smooth fudge with a knife, and then sprinkle with raw peanuts. Place in the fridge for 1 hour and cut into squares. Store in the refrigerator for best results.

Sauces, Rubs and Dressings (Maintenance) (10)

SMOKY BBQ SAUCE

2 TBSP sugar free tomato sauce
2–3 TBSP water
½ tsp dehydrated minced onion
½ tsp apple cider vinegar
¼ tsp sugar free Liquid Smoke
¼ tsp paprika
¼ tsp chili powder
1/8 tsp cinnamon
1/8 tsp cloves
¼ – ½ tsp stevia (if needed)
Salt/pepper to taste

In small non–stick saucepan, combine all ingredients and bring to boil. Reduce heat and simmer for 20 minutes. Makes enough for 1–2 servings.

EASY COCKTAIL SAUCE

½ c. sugar free catsup
1 TBSP Horseradish (drained)
1 tsp Lemon juice
1 TBSP Tomato paste

Mix in a bowl and place in refrigerator.

MAYO

1 Egg
2 TBSP Apple Cider Vinegar
2 TBSP Water
½ tsp sea salt
1/8 tsp each: pepper, onion powder and garlic powder
12–15 drops Liquid stevia
1 c. oil of choice

Mix egg, vinegar and water in blender, add spices and slowly add the oil while blender is running. Store for up to 3 days in the refrigerator.

BBQ SAUCE

3 ounces tomato paste
¼ c. apple cider vinegar
3 TBSP lemon juice
1 TBSP hot sauce
1 TBSP minced onion
3 cloves garlic, minced
¼ TSP chili powder
½ tsp garlic powder and onion powder
1 tsp chopped parsley
Stevia to taste (Dark chocolate liquid)
Cayenne pepper, salt and pepper to taste
Water, as needed to achieve desired consistency

In a small saucepan, combine all ingredients. Mix well and bring to a boil. Reduce heat and simmer for at least 5 minutes adding a little water to achieve desired consistency and to make sure it doesn't burn. Use as a barbeque sauce for chicken or beef.

THOUSAND ISLAND DRESSING

2 TBSP sugar free ketchup

2 TSP sugar free dill relish

1 ¼ c. sugar free mayo

Dash of garlic powder

1 TBSP vinegar

Stevia and pepper to taste

Mix all ingredients together. Place in the fridge and serve when cold.

BERRY SYRUP

½ c. strawberries

½ c. blueberries

½ c. water

1 tsp stevia

Place all items in a microwave-safe bowl. Microwave for 1–2 minutes, until berries are hot and a little mushy. Smash with spoon and serve. These are great for the crepes or Po' cakes.

YOUR HCG GREEK DRESSING

¼ c. olive oil

1 tsp dried oregano

Salt & pepper to taste

Place ingredients in a bowl, mix well, and use on your favorite salad choices.

ALFREDO SAUCE

½ c. unsalted butter
¾ c. grated Parmesan cheese
1 c. heavy cream
1 clove garlic, minced
1 tsp Italian seasoning

In a bowl, mix butter and cheese with an electric mixer until fluffy. Add cream slowly, until it's well mixed. Add garlic and Italian seasoning, and mix well. Place in a small saucepan over medium heat and cook until hot. Pour over spaghetti squash for a nice 'pasta' dish.

CHEESE SAUCE

1 c. heavy cream
½ c. water
2 c. shredded cheddar cheese
¼ tsp garlic salt
½ tsp dry mustard powder
¼ tsp paprika
¼ tsp onion powder

In a double boiler, add all ingredients. Stir frequently until smooth. Serve this warm over cauliflower or fish.

CHICKEN GRAVY

1 TBSP olive oil
2 lbs. chicken, cut up
½ c. chopped onion
½ c. fresh orange juice
¼ c. water
¼ tsp garlic powder
¼ tsp parsley

Heat oil in a frying pan over medium heat. Once oil is hot, add the chicken. When chicken is done, remove from pan. Place onion in frying pan, and cook until tender. Remove onion from pan. Stir in the orange juice and water into pan. Then add chicken and onion back into the frying pan. Cook over low heat and covered for 1 hour. If there doesn't look like there is enough gravy, add a little more orange juice.

Maintenance Phase

Now that you are done with the HCG drops, what do you do to maintain the weight loss? This phase is relatively simple. For 21 days immediately following the last day of the low calorie diet (Phase 2) you are allowed to eat as much food and any type of food you choose (provided it doesn't contain sugars, starches or any of the ingredients listed below). During the first 3–4 days on maintenance (Phase 3) watch out for protein deprivation. If you begin to gain weight it is likely due to insufficient protein. To resolve this issue, eat protein every 3 hours for 3–4 days. This will restock your protein supply and release the water weight. After the 1st three weeks of maintenance are over, you will slowly bring sugars and starches back into your diet for another 3 weeks. This will complete the maintenance phase. Please note that if you are doing multiple rounds of HCG, the maintenance phase will increase in length each time. Here is a chart for the length of maintenance after multiple rounds:

After round 1 – 6 weeks of maintenance
3 weeks of no sugars/starches followed by 3 weeks of SLOWLY reintroducing sugars/starches

After round 2 – 8 weeks of maintenance
4 weeks of no sugars/starches followed by 4 weeks of SLOWLY reintroducing sugars/starches

After round 3 – 12 weeks of maintenance
6 weeks of no sugars/starches followed by 6 weeks of
SLOWLY reintroducing sugars/starches

After round 4 – 20 weeks of maintenance
10 weeks of no sugars/starches followed by 10 weeks of
SLOWLY reintroducing sugars/starches

After round 5 – 6 months of maintenance
3 months of no sugars/starches followed by 3 months of
SLOWLY reintroducing sugars/starches

During the 1st half of maintenance you will want to avoid the following foods:

· No sugar, dextrose, sucrose, honey, molasses, high fructose corn syrup, corn syrup, maltodextrin, or any sweetener.

· No starch, including breads, pastas, any wheat product, white rice, potatoes, yams, beans, etc.

· No artificial sweeteners, including aspartame, sucralose, NutraSweet, Splenda, saccharin, etc.

· No food from fast food restaurants.

· No trans fats, including hydrogenated or partially hydrogenated oils (no processed foods).

· No nitrites.

· Limit non-prescription and prescription drug use.

You must absolutely weigh yourself every morning after first emptying your bladder. You must do this daily without fail. As it takes about three weeks after completing the low calorie diet before the weight stabilizes, it is important that daily weighing during this phase be continued. As long as your weight stays within two pounds of the weight reached on the day of the last drop, you are doing great. The moment the scale goes beyond two pounds, even by only a few ounces, you must do the following steps:

- The same day you notice the increase you must entirely skip all food until 6:00 p.m. During this time you should drink as much water, as you can, up to one gallon but at least 64 ounces. You must drink a minimum of half a gallon of pure water. In addition to the water, drink as much of the various teas that are recommended. In the evening eat the biggest steak you can from grass fed organic beef. The steak should be grilled and seasoned with pepper and salt, but nothing else. You may have either a large organic raw tomato or large organic raw apple.

It is of the utmost importance that these steps of skipping meals occur on the same day as the scale registered an increase of more than two pounds from the weight you achieved on the last day of the drops. You must not postpone this protocol until the following day. Weighing yourself daily is vitally important. Because the hypothalamus is now corrected from its abnormal condition, when you gain weight the body will not store the excess in the secure abnormal fat reserves. This means that weight gain will now result in storing of fat evenly throughout the body in the normal or structural fat areas. This means that by looking in the mirror, or by feeling how your clothes fit, it will be misleading. You can actually gain ten to fifteen pounds and never notice it. This is why daily weighing is so important.

During the first half of maintenance monitor and be aware of your appetite. Many people out of habit put large amounts of food on their plate. During this time you will notice you get full very quickly. Take note of the feeling of fullness and loss of appetite and stop eating! It is very important that you eat a full breakfast, lunch, and dinner, and have three snacks, ideally consisting of an organic apple or an organic grapefruit, however, during each meal it is advised that you eat slowly, consciously be aware of chewing your food thoroughly, and stop eating when you are full.

Many overweight people have the fear that if they don't continue to eat during mealtime they will be hungry later on and feel miserable. This 1st half of maintenance is important as it helps change behavioral habits that played a part in your weight. Some basic guidelines that will help change past behavioral habits that lead to obesity include the following:

- Sit at a table and be relaxed when eating a meal.
- Do not eat in front of the TV, in the car, or standing up.
- Eat slowly and consciously chew food thoroughly.
- Play relaxing music while eating.
- Put smaller amounts of food on your plate, and don't go for seconds.
- Be conscious about whether you are really hungry or full. Stop eating when you are no longer hungry, but feel full and satisfied.

You should never gain more than two pounds during this phase without immediately correcting this situation by doing the steak day protocol. Surprisingly, Simeons discovered that it is equally undesirable for you to lose more than two pounds after the last drop. This is because any loss of weight after the last drop is usually a loss of muscle, or structural fat.

Simeons noted that some patients become overly enthusiastic after the success they achieved during the low calorie diet. These patients do not believe they can eat normal amounts of food six times per day without regaining weight. They disregard the advice to eat anything they please (with the short list of exceptions) and want to play it safe. They try, more or less, to continue the low calorie diet with minor variations. To their horror they find that their weight actually goes up. They then follow the instructions of skipping breakfast and lunch, but are afraid to eat the steak for fear of gaining more weight and instead have something such as a small salad. They become hungry and weak. The next morning they find they've increased yet another pound! They feel terrible and even the dreaded swelling of their ankles comes back. Dr. Simeons explained this phenomenon in these terms. During treatment the patient is just above the verge of protein deficiency, but because of the HCG, protein is being fed back into a system from the breakdown and release of the secure problem area fatty tissue. Once the treatment is over, there is no more HCG in the body and this process no longer takes place. Unless an adequate amount of protein is eaten as soon as treatment is over, protein deficiency is bound to develop. This inevitably caused a marked retention of water, increased weight, which many times results in swelling of the ankles, huge hunger, tiredness, and irritability.

It is advised that you follow these instructions exactly as described. Never do this or any weight loss program without being supervised by a licensed health care practitioner.

Low Calorie Diet Meal Planner

	Breakfast	Lunch	Dinner
Day 1 Load Day	English Muffin with bacon, egg & cheese	Pasta with Alfredo sauce, breadsticks and salad with full fat dressing	Pork chops, rice, vegetables with butter and rolls with butter
Day 2 Load Day	Pancakes with butter and syrup, sausage, eggs and hash browns	Fast Food Lunch	Beef stroganoff, served with buttered rolls and buttered vegetables
Day 3	Coffee and Tea	Salad with chicken breast & apple cider vinegar dressing with Melba toast and an orange	Southern Style Greens and Spicy 'Fried' Chicken with Strawberries and Melba toast
Day 4	Coffee and Tea	Sweet N Spicy Chicken Wraps with Grapefruit and Melba toast	Blackened Chicken Salad with Melba toast
Day 5	Coffee and Tea	Melba Delight with Strawberries	Cucumber Dill Salad with Cinnamon Beef, an orange and Melba toast
Day 6	Coffee and Tea	Hot & Sour Shrimp Soup with Melba toast and an apple	Lemon Mustard Chicken with Onion Rings and Melba toast served with Cinnamon Spiced Grapefruit
Day 7	Coffee and Tea	Asian Salad	Wasabi White Fish with Lemon Ginger Asparagus, Melba toast and Strawberries
Day 8	Coffee and Tea	Radish Soup with Melba toast and grapefruit	Breaded Chicken 'Tenders' and salad with vinaigrette dressing and an apple
Day 9	Coffee and Tea	Chopped Chicken Salad with Strawberries	Rock Lobster with asparagus, Melba toast and an orange

Day 10	Coffee and Tea	Strawberry Whey Protein Shake with Lettuce and HCG dressing & Melba toast	YourHCG.com Stew with Cinnamon Applesauce
Day 11	Coffee and Tea	YourHCG.com Taco Salad with Chicken and Orange	Curry Shrimp served with Tangy Crunchy Cabbage and Grapefruit
Day 12	Coffee and Tea	Meatballs with Roasted Asparagus and Strawberries	Oven Fried Garlic Chicken with Onion Rings and Apple
Day 13	Coffee and Tea	Lemon Chicken Soup with Melba toast and orange	Cajun Shrimp Kabobs with Roasted Garlic Asparagus and Strawberries and Crème
Day 14	Coffee and Tea	Wasabi White Fish with Lemon Ginger Asparagus, Melba toast and apple	Cream of Chicken Soup with Melba toast and Grapefruit
Day 15	Coffee and Tea	Orange Vanilla Shake	Southern Style Greens with Spicy 'Fried' Chicken and Strawberries
Day 16	Coffee and Tea	Radish Soup with Melba toast and Grapefruit	Breaded Chicken 'Tenders' and Salad with Vinaigrette Dressing served with Your HCG Apple Cobbler
Day 17	Coffee and Tea	Blackened Chicken Salad with Melba toast and Strawberries	Boneless Hot Wings with Celery, Melba toast and orange
Day 18	Coffee and Tea	Strawberry Whey Protein Shake with celery	Melba Delight
Day 19	Coffee and Tea	Italian Beef Soup with Melba toast and Orange	Your HCG.com Cioppino with Melba toast and Grapefruit

Day 20	Coffee and Tea	Curry Shrimp served with Tangy Crunchy Cabbage and Strawberries	Hot & Sour Shrimp Soup with Melba toast and Apple
Day 21	Coffee and Tea	Orange Vanilla Shake with Cucumbers	Lemon Chicken Soup with Melba toast and Strawberries
Day 22	Coffee and Tea	French Onion Soup with Melba toast and Apple	Rock Lobster with Asparagus, Melba toast and Grapefruit
Day 23	Coffee and Tea	Boneless Hot Wings with Celery, Melba toast and Orange	Chopped Chicken Salad with Vanilla Strawberry Dessert
Day 24	Coffee and Tea	Cajun Shrimp Kabobs with Asparagus and Grapefruit	Blackened Chicken Salad with Melba toast and Apple
Day 25	Coffee and Tea	Cabbage Wraps with Strawberries	Creole Shrimp with Tangy Crunchy Cabbage and Orange
Day 26	Coffee and Tea	Spicy Crab Cucumber Salad with Apple	Kung Pao Chicken with Melba Toast served with Your HCG.com 'Pie' with strawberries
Day 27	Coffee and Tea	Breaded Chicken 'Tenders' and salad with vinaigrette dressing and Orange	Inside Out French Dip with Onion Rings, Melba toast and Grapefruit
Day 28	Coffee and Tea	Cucumber Shrimp Salad with Melba toast	Orange Ginger Chicken with Melba toast and Strawberry Sorbet
Day 29	Coffee and Tea	Sweet N Spicy Chicken Wraps with Orange	Lemon Pepper Fish, Asparagus and Strawberries
Day 30	Coffee and Tea	Shish Kabobs, Melba toast and Apple	Cabbage Wraps with Grapefruit
Day 31 No Drops	Coffee and Tea	Chopped Chicken Salad with Orange	French Onion Soup with Melba toast and Warm Cinnamon Apple

Day 32 No Drops	Coffee and Tea	YourHCG.com Taco Salad with Chicken and Apple	Lemon Oregano Fish with Steamed Spinach, Melba toast and Strawberries
Day 33 No Drops	Coffee and Tea	Strawberry Whey Protein Shake with Celery	Melba Delight with Orange and Melba toast

Weight Tracking Chart

This weight-tracking chart is a great tool to keep track of both the pounds and inches that you are losing. It's a good idea to weigh yourself daily. This should be done in the morning, when you wake up, after you go to the bathroom, and after you have disrobed. This will ensure there is no variation in your weight due to clothing or a full bladder. Measure the inches lost each week. This does not need to be done daily. Here is the proper way to measure inches:

CHEST – Measure the fullest part of your chest.
WAIST – Measure the narrowest part of your stomach, about 1 inch above the belly button.
HIPS – Measure around the fullest part of your butt with your heels together.
THIGHS – Measure right under your pubic bone on your thigh. This should be the fullest part of your thigh.
ARMS – Measure around your arm, starting about half way between your elbow and armpit.

Date	Weight	Chest	Waist	Hips	Right	Left	Right	Left
6/1/11	190lbs	44	37	47	23	23	12	12
Day 1 Load Day	245							
Day 2 Load Day	243							
Day 3	240							
Day 4								
Day 5								
Day 6								
Day 7	231.5							

1/20

1/26

	Day								
	Day 8								
	Day 9								
	Day 10	228.5							
1/30	Day 11	229							
1/31	Day 12	227							
2/1	Day 13	226							
	Day 14								
	Day 15								
	Day 16								
	Day 17								
	Day 18								
2/7	Day 19	225							
8	Day 20								
9	Day 21								
10	Day 22								
11	Day 23								
12	Day 24	222.5							
13	Day 25	221.5							
14	Day 26								
15	Day 27								
16	Day 28								
17	Day 29								
2/18	Day 30								
19	Day 31 No Drops								
20	Day 32 No Drops	221.5							
21	Day 33 No Drops								

Food Journal

Date	Breakfast	Lunch	Dinner	Water in Ounces
Day 1 Load Day				
Day 2 Load Day				
Day 3				
Day 4				
Day 5				
Day 6				
Day 7				
Day 8				
Day 9				
Day 10				
Day 11				

Day 12				
Day 13				
Day 14				
Day 15				
Day 16				
Day 17				
Day 18				
Day 19				
Day 20				
Day 21				
Day 22				
Day 23				
Day 24				

Day 25				
Day 26				
Day 27				
Day 28				
Day 29				
Day 30				
Day 31 No Drops				
Day 32 No Drops				
Day 33 No Drops				